dent
drive

ONE STREET. FOUR YEARS. LIFELONG FRIENDSHIPS.

Dent Drive: One Street. Four Years. Lifelong Friendships.

First names are included with consent of characters. Last names have been removed to uphold confidentiality.

Written by Tania Farran, Carol Barrale-Roettger, Rob Barrale
Book design by Kristen Landon, Maddie Villeneuve, Alexis Romeril
Contributions by Annika Farran
Edited by Maddie Villeneuve

Published by Creative Living Ideas
ISBN: 978-1-7363567-2-2
www.creativelivingideas.com

To my dear friends - Thank you to my friends on Dent Drive! Who would have known we would create forever friendships? You will always be my friends. You have no idea how much that short time with you all has impacted my life. I love you.

To my mom and brother - Thank you for collaborating with me on this book. It was so much fun to relive these moments together and put them down on paper forever. I feel so blessed to have you in my life and to have lived together in the 70's in sunny San Diego. What a time. I love you.

To my husband - You always encourage me to follow my dreams! Your support and love keeps me thriving. I am so happy to have you by my side. I love you.

To my girls - May you cherish the friendships you have made. They are precious. I know that you both have found forever friends, and it is the best thing in the world. Thank you for being such wonderful daughters. I love you.

To my CLI team - You have helped make my dreams come true. Thank you so very much! Your brilliant work and dedication are amazing. I love you too.

Tania

Introduction

It had been a decade since I'd been back to the place I lived as a child — Dent Drive, San Diego, California. The place that always makes my heart happy. The place I made forever friends. The place that left a lasting impact on my life. But my heart felt heavy when I finally decided to return to Dent Drive. So much time had passed since I had actually laid eyes on the old neighborhood and my dear friends.

My mom and I made the trip in March of 2020. We had been discussing the trip for the last couple of years, but life got in the way. Before we knew it, 10 years had gone by, and we hadn't made the trip. Don't get me wrong — life was busy. Raising kids and working full-time can really cramp a person's style. My mother had battled and survived cancer twice in those years, which added to the travel difficulties. But in August of 2019, my friend Stacy lost her father to ALS. It was a very quick diagnosis. His death was the first of our parents on the street. It was tragic and hit me with a huge dose of reality. I knew then that life wasn't going to be like this forever. I needed to get back to California as soon as I could.

I decided that my mom and I would take a quick trip over spring break. I had given the traditional sentiments to Stacy and Jane (Stacy's mother) about the passing of Sas. I sent a nice gift and expressed my condolences, but it just wasn't enough for me. I needed to feel them in

6

my arms, hug them tight, and cry with them. I needed them to know that I was feeling pain and sorrow, much like they were. Jane had suffered a stroke a few years prior and was still struggling with her speech. Life was moving quickly for my dear friend, and I wanted to be there to give her support. I needed to see Stacy, my "kindergarten friend" (even though we didn't actually go to kindergarten together), my forever friend.

Our lives had changed over the course of time, and I was anxious to get back with the people that I enjoyed so much. Forty-five years ago, I don't think we knew where this adventure called life was going to take us. Back then, we didn't know that we were creating lifelong friendships on Dent Drive. We didn't know that our friendships would last through so many of life's challenges: divorces, children with disabilities, aging parents, deaths in the family. Going home in March of 2020 was particularly challenging, as I was faced with the reality that the place I once called home was not going to be the same. We had great childhood times on Dent Drive, so many wonderful memories from such a short time. But we children now have our own grown children. As our families were growing, our parents were aging. Our childhood friendships had stayed the course for years, but time was passing. I knew it was time to return. And I knew that we would all get together and pick right back up where we left off. Spending time laughing and reminiscing always begins right away when you reunite with forever friends.

We lived on a street that had kids in every house. For the most part, we all got along. We moved to Dent Drive in 1975: my parents, Bob and Carol; my older brother, Robbie; and I. Next door to us was Sas and Jane and their two kids, Stacy and Bret. They were close in age to my brother and I. Stacy and Bret became our closest friends on the street because we went to school together. Joan and John, along with their three kids, Mike, Cynthia, and Holly, lived across the street from us. Mike and Cyn were in high school. Holly was my brother's age. There were other kids on the street, but our three families really stayed connected over the years.

As I walked down Dent Drive in 2020, my mind was flooded with memories. I could literally hear the voices of my childhood friends from the past. I could see the games being played on the street and in the yards. I could see the families doing their day-to-day, 70's activities: washing their cars, mowing their lawns, kids riding bikes, barking dogs, and the beautiful sun shining through the palm trees. Everything looked the same, yet everything was different. I took a video walking down the street to keep it close to me forever. That afternoon I went back to the hotel room while my mom stayed and had tea with her friends. I needed some time alone to process the strong emotions I was feeling. I ended up calling my husband, sobbing. He listened and told me to enjoy these moments and all the happy memories that came with them. I was not sad; my heart was just filled with so much love and emotion. Revisiting the special memories that I get to remember forever was overwhelming and incredible.

This was such an iconic time in my life. The memories I made with my friends are priceless. Back in 1975, we played outside all day long. We only came home when our parents called our names (or when my mom whistled). We solved our own problems; it was survival of the fittest at its finest. Back in the 70's, life was great. To be a five-year-old in the 70's in one of the most beautiful cities in the United States...what a time and place to grow up. I don't think I knew how lucky I was to live there.

Tania

The Arrival to San Diego

When we arrived in San Diego, Robbie was eight, and I was five. My parents were young and in their late 20's. My dad, who was a police officer back in St. Louis, had just taken a job with the Naval Investigative Service (NIS) in San Diego, California. He had the perfect look for the job — black, wavy hair and a thick, black mustache. Just like a detective on a 70's crime show. My mom was a blonde beauty with her long hair parted down the middle. They both donned bell bottom pants and wide-collared shirts, the epitome of the era. Mom had been working at JC Penney's back in St. Louis, so she had to quit her job to make the move. She didn't have any job leads in San Diego yet. Talk about a brave move. My parents were young and carefree. They just knew everything would turn out fine. But maybe they were also just young enough to not know what they should be worried about.

When we moved from St. Louis to San Diego in 1975, I didn't really understand what that meant. I just knew that we were moving, and my parents were both excited and sad. Looking back, I can't imagine being brave enough to just load up the kids and head out west like the pioneers. A co-worker of my father's picked out the house my parents would rent. Can you imagine? Moving into a home you have never laid eyes on? There was no Internet or Facetime to tour the home. There was no Zillow to help out either. Talk about trusting someone with your life. Fortunately, it turned out marvelously.

My parents loaded up our entire home into a single moving truck. We didn't take any other vehicles with us; it was just us and the truck. The brave belief that life would be great in sunny San Diego fueled the trip. How we got a car when we arrived was beyond me. My mom said a tearful goodbye to our grandparents and friends from our front yard in St. Louis. I can only imagine how my grandparents felt about us conservative Midwesterners heading across the country to where the hippies lived. The trip took us three days. All four of us rode in the cab of the moving truck. I rode the entire trip on my mom's lap. Could you imagine driving like that nowadays? With a five-year-old on your lap? My, how times have changed. There were no iPhones, tablets, or DVD players to entertain us. I can't imagine how our parents kept us occupied the entire time. I do remember singing "Three Little Fishes" and "Possie the Two Gun Cowboy" countless times. These were songs my grandparents taught me, and my mom encouraged me to sing with her to pass the time. We must have played the alphabet game too. I don't remember being miserable on the journey, so my parents definitely made the trip enjoyable somehow.

When we arrived in San Diego, I remember getting out of the truck and looking around at my new surroundings. With my pigtails and Rub-A-Dub doll (this was a doll I loved; you could take her in the bathtub with you), my five-year-old self took it all in. The sky was blue and beautiful. Our home was a modest three-bedroom ranch painted a light green color. It was on the corner of a street and had a palm tree in the yard. Our neighbors came out to meet us, and I realized that there was a little girl close to my age who lived right next door. I was happy about that. Her name was Stacy, and she was a petite little girl with long arms and long legs. She had pigtails just like me, and she had the same dolly as me too. Her mom introduced us and pointed out the fact that we had the same doll. She was a year younger than me, but the moment I arrived we instantly had something in common — our Rub-A-Dub dolly. Looking back, she was quite possibly the ugliest doll anyone could ever have. But it was the first thing Stacy and I connected over.

Stacy's parents were Jane and Sas, a Japanese couple who spoke very little Japanese (probably none to be honest with you). Jane made the best Mexican food. She flipped everything with chopsticks (even pancakes), which I remember amazed me. Jane had gorgeous black hair and a giggle and snicker that made you do the same. Her laughter was contagious and always made everyone end up giggling. Sas was a giant — a very tall man with a wonderful smile. He was such a gentle and patient man. Stacy smiled and giggled when we met each other. Now, my mom will tell you that it was the first time she met an Asian person, but as a child I didn't even notice that Stacy and I looked different. That is the beauty of childhood; it's a time of innocence and open-mindedness. Little did I know, we would become great friends and spend countless days together. Stacy's brother, Bret, was a year younger than my brother. Bret was hilarious, impulsive, and fearless. Unless he was really afraid, in which case, he was petrified. The adventures that Robbie and Bret had together were probably just as laughable as the ones Stacy and I enjoyed.

We met our other neighbors that day too. Joanie and John lived across the street and had three children. Joanie had a hearty laugh and could find a solution to any problem. John was a college teacher — a bit of a nerd and proud of it. The pair were two of the funniest people I ever met. They were always so progressive with technology. They had the latest and greatest electronics and appliances. They had the first microwave I ever saw. It was huge! I remember being amazed. Mike, Cynthia, and Holly were their children, and they were the epitome of Southern California. They were blonde, tan, and totally cool! Mike was ever adventurous. He was older than us and seemed to spend most of his time at the beach. He was the typical Southern California beach boy: a tan, beach-loving, Mexican-poncho-wearing guy. Cynthia, who was also older than us, was always dressed in her hip bell bottoms. She was tan with blonde hair. The siblings were definitely living the California dream or at least I thought they were in 1975. They had sailboats in their yard and went to the beach all the time. They called their parents by their first names; that was a new one for me! Holly was the same age as my brother and was a cute little blonde with a sweet giggle and a huge smile. As I reflect now, I wonder if they came out to see the country bumpkins arriving from Missouri. Did the Clampetts just arrive in California? Little did I know, they were the least judgmental and most loving neighbors anyone could ask for.

It was the 70's in San Diego. The days of Ditto jeans, Hello Kitty, Donny and Marie, and *Grease*! Barbies were all the rage. Kids played outside all day long. We played in the street and drank out of the garden hose. We rode bikes in the rain and jumped rope in the sunshine. We layed in the grass and stained our knees. We went to the beach, fed the seagulls, and burned our skin. *The Love Boat*, *Charlie's Angels*, *Fantasy Island*, and *CHIPS* were on TV. Cartoons played only on Saturday mornings (if you slept in, you missed them). Abbot and Costello were on the Saturday Matinee. Nothing was on demand. Life was good!

Carol

Moving to California: A Perfect Fit

Oh my gosh! It's a perfect fit! An absolute perfect fit! I'm not talking about a dress, a pair of shoes, or a hat. I'm not even talking about a chair. I'm talking about the day we were backing up the moving truck into the driveway in September of 1975. You know how the weather is out there…as they say in San Diego, "Everyday is another day in paradise." Sunshine, blue skies, temperatures in the 70's — yep, paradise.

As we were unloading the truck, the kids were so excited. They were scurrying in and out of the new home, finding their bedrooms. Robbie was eight, and Tania was turning six in January. Tania was dragging around her Rub-A-Dub doll. On the side of the house by a big Yucca tree, a Japanese woman appeared standing next to our truck. I stopped in my tracks. This may be a revelation to the younger generation, but I had never had a face-to-face experience or conversation with a Japanese person in my life! I was very surprised! She was the friendliest sort of lady I had ever met, and she greeted me with a great big smile. Later I would find out that her heart was 10 times bigger than her smile. She addressed the children right away, asking them how old they were and telling Tania that her daughter had a Rub-A-Dub doll too. She informed Robbie that she had a son who was a year younger and confirmed that they would have so much fun together.

After a few moments, the lady who lived across the street came over to check things out. She introduced herself as Joanie and pointed to her home. Meeting Joanie, I thought, "Hmm…She has sailboats (not just one, but two catamarans) in her front yard! Now that's interesting." At the time, I didn't know what type of boats they were, I just saw the big sails up. Newsflash — none of my neighbors in Missouri had sailboats in their yard. It was a little surprising to say the least.

So within a half hour of backing our moving truck up to the garage, we had met Jane, the Japanese lady, and Joanie, the lady who had sailboats in her yard. They would wind up being my BESTIES!

Joanie explained that she had three children: two older than Robbie and one older than Tania. Joanie and Jane were extremely friendly ladies. They later confessed they were very curious to see what type of people were moving into Dent Drive. Just checking out the newbies.

As we visited and shared pleasantries for a while, Jane suddenly yelled out, "Oh, oh! RYAN!" She turned and ran, lickety-split, into her home.

That's when Joanie started laughing and calmly said, "Jane forgot she's babysitting Ryan. He's 18 months old." We both began to laugh. I suspected that we, "the New Family," had been approved and accepted as members of the Dent Drive Gang!

That was the beginning of a 45-year relationship that I cherish with my whole heart. I have expressed to Jane and Joanie how much I appreciate them, not just for opening up their neighborhood friendship to us, but also allowing us to be in their homes, their families, and their hearts going forward.

A few years ago, I purchased a sign. I gave it to my granddaughter who was in college in Chicago and about 19 years old at the time. She was struggling with being away from home.

The sign said, "HOME is not a place but a FEELING."

That's what I got, that feeling, when I moved my family 1,792 miles away from St. Louis. We left behind their grandparents, their schools, our families, and our friends. But these two wonderful ladies and their families gave me the confidence and support to know things were going to be alright. And what a perfect fit it was!

Rob

Taking the Northern Route

In 1975, we made the move from St. Louis to San Diego in a yellow moving truck. I was eight, and Tania was five. We were living in St. Louis, where my parents grew up and my four grandparents lived. All of the grandparents came over to our house to help us pack up the rented box truck. I had already started third grade and don't remember being upset about having to leave. I was more excited about the adventure ahead of us. I remember my mom and the grandparents getting emotional as we said our last goodbyes. All four of us hopped into the cab of the manual transmission, no air conditioning, AM radio truck. We were supposed to be towing our Chrysler Sedan, but no one could figure out how to hook the tow bar up to the hitch of the moving truck. So after many attempts, we left the Sedan behind. We left it right there on the side of the road by our old house. My grandparents ended up selling it for a few hundred dollars.

So, off we went — headed for San Diego via the Northern route across Kansas and through Colorado. I remember us driving through the mountains so slowly, getting passed by every vehicle heading west. My dad would say, "We have to put it in granny gear," as he downshifted all the way into first. To keep us kids occupied, my mom led us in a few songs, such as, "Row, Row, Row Your Boat." But the one that sticks out decades later is the countless times we sang the "Three Little Fishies" song. It was Tania's favorite. All these years later, I can still remember the lyrics: "Swim, said the momma fish, swim if you can. And they swam and they swam all over the dam. Boop, boop, dittem, dattem, wattem, chu." Part of the fun was being able to say "dam" without repercussions!

The trip took two long days, but we finally made it to San Diego. My parents had rented a house on Dent Drive that was valued at $50,000 after selling our home in St. Louis for $16,000, which was the first indication of the tremendous difference in cost of living between our old city and our new one. I don't remember pulling up to our new house, but I do remember marveling at the palm trees, the small yards, and the rocks where grass should have been. The landscape had a brown hue, which was something we weren't used to coming from St. Louis. We even had one of those palm trees in OUR yard!

I remember the first time I saw Bret, who would later become one of my best friends. He was riding his Big Wheel in his driveway. He was seven at the time, one year younger than me. He was immediately engaging and friendly. Dent Drive had a lot of incredible experiences in store for us.

Tania

Magnificent Moms

Jane, Joanie, and my mom (Carol) became fast friends in the 70's and remained friends throughout the years. They spent many mornings in the good old days visiting over coffee and tea. During our most recent trip to San Diego, we were having afternoon tea in Jane's kitchen. It had been remodeled with a new floor and countertops but still resembled the same kitchen where Stacy and I would eat from our Hello Kitty rice bowls with matching chopsticks. Standing in that same kitchen made me wonder what they really talked about each day when we would go outside to play or head off to school. We were kids, just going about our business. They were mothers, wives, women who had lives of their own. So I decided to ask them what they talked about all those years ago.

"You know what I really want to know?" I asked.

"What do you want to know?" replied my mom.

I said, "I want to know what you three talked about each day after we left for school."

The three of them giggled and then Joanie said, "Oh you know…we just talked about this and that."

I told them I didn't believe them; I would have loved to be a fly on the wall during those mornings. I bet there was some serious gossip going on. As we drank our tea, the sly looks and subtle grins continued between the three moms. My mom finally said, "Well, I do remember when Joanie brought a friend down to meet us for tea one day." They then proceeded to tell me about the time Joanie brought a neighbor to tea. The minute she arrived she wanted to share some very exciting news. She had gotten breast implants! Remember — this was the 70's, and I think breast implants were a very new concept. My mom was a modest young woman from the Midwest. They remember this lady very openly showing her breasts to them! My mom remarked that she was shocked, and she said that Jane's eyes almost popped out of her head. The three of them just laughed and laughed, remembering how embarrassed my mom was at the time. While reminiscing, my mom said, "I remember thinking 'Oh my gosh, what kind of neighbors were on this street?'"

As a child in the 70's, I didn't pay much attention to the fact that they became fast friends. I remember that Joanie rarely had shoes on and often wore a flowered gown to cross the street over to Jane's house. She would walk right into the house with a verbal, "Knock, knock." My mom would join in by walking straight into Jane's house too. I don't think our doors were ever locked. I'm not sure if any days went by where they did not see each other.

Stained Glass Shenanigans

During the time we lived on Dent Drive, the three moms took a stained glass class together. Joanie is a very handy, crafty lady, and I think she often lured the other two into her brilliant ideas. Jane is very meticulous in any crafting that she does. If Jane makes a bow for a gift, it will take her 30 minutes because it has to be perfect. On the other hand, my mom is not a perfectionist. She likes to giggle, chit-chat, and have fun. So as the story goes…

They were in stained glass class working on some majestic works of art. I'm sure the three ladies were creating something really 70's, like a powder blue stained glass planter to hang on the wall (which would, of course, hold your spider plant). In fact, I still have the planter my mom made that day. It is as cute as ever but not perfect. Mine is powder blue and my brother's is yellow, his favorite color. During the class, my mom was talking away and the instructor, Joel, was trying to teach. They distinctly remembered his name, so this moment must've been impactful. Joel asked my mom to quiet down, but she did not. Go figure — my mother not being quiet. Well he must have had enough at some point because he chucked the blackboard eraser at my mother! It may be hard to believe, but if you know her, you won't be surprised. Jane and Joanie still giggle about how Carol got in trouble at stained glass class. My mom loves to laugh and have a good time. She doesn't take life too seriously, and sometimes it catches up with her.

Crafts Galore

When Stacy, Holly, and I were young girls, we had the luxury of our parents working together to create some of the greatest craft projects ever. In California, houses do not have basements, so most people use their garage as they would a basement. Our garage held our washer and dryer, toys, bikes and a big table for crafts. Notice there were no cars in the garage; they stayed in the driveway. I remember Jane using her dining room table as her crafting area. These ladies made us many homemade goods from their work spaces.

Wrap-Around Shorts

In the 70's, wrap-around shorts were the thing! You had to put them on like a diaper by tying them in the back, pulling them through your legs, wrapping them around your waist, and tying them in the front. All the girls on Dent Drive wanted them. Joanie was so handy that instead of buying patterns for everyone in their size, she was able to create the pattern from a grocery bag. I remember my mind being blown. Joanie always found an easier way of doing things. Nonchalantly, she would say, "I can do it." And voila, the shorts were created. She was like a magician. All the girls on Dent Drive had them in Hawaiian floral patterns. We absolutely loved them. They made going to the bathroom a bit tricky, but we managed just fine!

Dance Costumes

Stacy and I took tap class at our elementary's after-school program. We performed in an auditorium complete with a stage. It was a small room, but it seemed huge when I was practicing as a child. It was the first extracurricular class I had taken. Stacy and I were in different age groups for our recitals, but our classes and warm ups took place in the same gym. Stacy was so petite but had long arms and legs. They were floppy when she danced, but she was a carefree kiddo anyway. She would just giggle and shuffle-ball-change her way around the stage. We both loved singing and dancing, which was another connection for the two of us! I must've been in first grade while she was in kindergarten because we had different costumes for our recitals. For some reason, I remember her routine and costume to this day. It was "Animal Crackers in My Soup," and she wore a white halter jumpsuit printed with zoo animals. I remember my mom and Jane sewing sequins on our costumes for days leading up to our recitals. Jane had these great chairs in her living room that swiveled. I remember our moms sitting in those chairs, sewing sequins on our costumes, talking, laughing, and parenting. I have no idea how long the costumes really took them, but it seemed like forever. Maybe they took their time because they just enjoyed the time together.

For 45 years, these ladies stayed connected regardless of life's trials and tribulations. They have raised families and supported each other along the way. When my mom was diagnosed with ovarian cancer in 2008, I remember the outpouring of love from these women. Flowers were sent and phone calls were made regularly. When Jane had a stroke, they continued to stay connected and increased their support for her. Joanie (still being Jane's neighbor) checks on her regularly. Jane's husband, Sas, was diagnosed with ALS in 2019 and passed away that August. Again, the ladies rallied around each other to support Jane. My mom supported Jane from St. Louis, as best as she could from such a distance. To this day, their connection and support for one another is unbreakable.

Rob

Kids Next Door

The 70's were the days when everything was "bitchin," "radical," "totally awesome," or "totally rad." Of course we used these terms, but Bret had an even more unique vocabulary. He'd say, "Hi, Scary," to anyone he thought looked odd, like the lady with the big hair who pulled up next to us at a stoplight. He'd say, "Hi, Geri," to older people, which is funny that a kid was referring to older adults as geriatrics.

Bret had a slender athletic build and like all of us at the time was as tan as Southern California allowed. Bret was trustworthy and silly at the same time. When we would go out and his mom would try to take pictures, he'd say, "Awh, mom, that's totally tourist." He would be so embarrassed. I also remember Bret repeatedly singing a car dealer's slogan ("Pete Ellis, what a great, great guy") after we got the red Ford Mercury. It was a cool looking car, but it wasn't great, so we called it the Red Lemon. Bret would re-write the words of the slogan and sing his own version, calling the dealer, "Pete Ellis, what a bad, bad guy" for selling us that car. He had unlimited energy — just eating dinner was a test of his patience. He would sit partially on his chair with one leg out ready to dash!

Stacy, Bret's little sister, sported the "Mindy" hairstyle from Mork and Mindy (just like all the rest of the girls on Dent Drive). She would practice piano every day. Our house was so close to theirs that you could easily hear her playing in her family room from our kitchen. Our houses couldn't have been more than 6 or 7 feet apart, so her practicing was a daily soundtrack in our house.

Tania and Stacy were in Campfire Girls, which was an organization similar to Girl Scouts. Their annual fundraiser was selling cans of peanuts. Bret and I would go out with Tania and Stacy (Bret with Tania, me with Stacy), pull the wagons, and keep an eye on the sales efforts. We would compete to see who could sell more between the two groups, but I don't remember who won.

Mike rode a unicycle, and he was really good at it. He would just ride it up and down Dent Drive, not a care in the world. I tried it a few times but never could get it figured out. He also made a super magnifying glass by mounting a concave piece of glass on a piece of wood that swiveled. That thing was so powerful you could burn paper or leaves with it.

Some of the other neighborhood boys would roll up newspapers, fill their mouths with flour, light the newspapers on fire, and then blow the flour through the newspapers — a la the human torch circus act!

Jeff was a year older than me and looked the part of a California teen. He stood a bit taller, was a little more athletic, and was beginning to be interested in girls. I remember days going over to his house when he would still be in bed and we would hang out listening to the newest vinyl album by the Police.

Keith B. lived directly behind us. He had strawberry blond hair, and he was the most conscientious one of us all. He was the one who would be first to ask how things were going or if you needed any help. Kind of like the morale leader. He was the one to say, "Hey. It's ok to go inside and go to the bathroom. We'll wait for you," when one of the younger neighborhood kids had to go to the bathroom badly and didn't want to miss out on the game of the day.

Keith H. and John H. were brothers who lived directly across the street with their sisters Lynn and Christine. They had plastic runners in their hallways and a fun pastime was to turn them over so the pointy nubs faced up for their unsuspecting guests or sisters. Keith, John, and Christine were accomplished Karate students advancing far up the belt chain. I once saw Keith quickly disengage a teenager from another neighborhood kid who was causing problems with two Karate kicks. It happened so fast that the other teen was dumbfounded, did not say a word, and left. This was the only near physical altercation I can remember from all of those years on Dent Drive, and it lasted less than a few minutes. I don't remember what the issue was originally, but I knew that Keith was justified in his action. Keith never flaunted his skills, and he knew from his teachings to only engage when absolutely necessary.

The two Keiths were two years older than me and were deemed "cool" primarily because they were older. Keith H. and John were altar boys at the same Catholic church that we attended. One Sunday I was in line for communion, and Keith was holding the brass plate under each parishioner's chin to catch any wayward communion wafers. When it was my turn, he subtly pushed the plate against my neck and gave me that look a friend gives when they are messing with you.

Steven lived in "centerfield," or just off of the cul-de-sac. He was younger and smaller than the rest of us. Just like everyone else, he was nice and always wanted to play outside when he could. He had two older brothers who had driver's licenses, so we rarely saw them around. As I remember it, one of his older brothers was working at a pizza parlor and inadvertently mixed ammonia and bleach while cleaning the floor and was overcome by the fumes. He made a full recovery, but it was one of those events that is a life lesson I remember to this day.

Gratia lived on Jackie, but only a house off of Dent Drive. She played with the girls because, in those days, the boys and girls did their own things. While I rarely interacted with Gratia, unbeknownst to her, she became the root of several years of teasing within my family. One day when my aunt and uncle were visiting us from St. Louis, I was out back playing kickball with my uncle. Gratia was walking down Jackie and yelled over the fence, "Robbie, that is my ball, but you can play with it!" Well, that was all my uncle needed to tease me that day, week, and many years into the future…

There were a few kids up the street that went by the names "Gas" and "Mugs." I'm not sure if that was their initials or not. They didn't play with us much, but I remember the unique nicknames.

The older kids (Mark and Scott, as I recall) would make what we called a Montana Goose Gun. It was made out of metal tennis ball containers held together by an excessive amount of duct tape. Lighter fluid was added through a hole in the bottom, and the gun was lit. The tennis balls would shoot out of it like it was a cannon. Bret and I kept a safe distance from these, but we still watched it all happen.

I have a few specific memories of Tania that stand out. Like the day she was brushing Rub-A-Dub dolly's hair and her head fell right off her shoulders. Tania screamed as loud as I can ever recall. Almost every New Year's Eve, I think of one of our New Year's Eves in San Diego. We were waiting up for the ball to drop in NYC, and Tania was having a hard time staying awake. She finally exclaimed, "Why can't they make New Year's Eve earlier for us little kids?"

Carol

Groundhog Day

We moved in September of 1975, and it was very hot. I thought Southern California was supposed to be hot...ya know, bikinis and all that. But, I wasn't acclimated to the dry heat and didn't know about the Santa Ana Winds. The extreme winds off the Santa Ana Dessert blew in every fall (not that I knew that then).

As we got settled, I had my moments of homesickness. The kids got settled in their school. I unpacked all the boxes and figured out where the grocery stores were. The house was clean, and the laundry was done. Now what? I remember sitting in silence and waiting for half-day kindergarten to be over, so I could have lunch with Tania. At this time, I wasn't best buds with Jane and Joanie yet. We were all still testing the waters in the new neighborhood. I wrote letters home to both sets of parents.

Dear Mom and Dad,
       All is good! Kids are great! Weather is wonderful. Miss you.
              Hope all is good with everyone back home.
                            Love,
                            Carol, Bob, Robbie, and Tania

Back in the 70's, long distance calls were put through an operator, so it was too expensive to call home more than once a week. That long distance phone call was always saved for the weekends, so everyone in the family could say, "Hi!" You know the phone that was tied to the wall and had a rotary dial with a 6-10 foot cord from the receiver to the wall? That long, curly cord stretched quite a bit, so you could reach a chair to sit while you talked.

Robbie came home around three. It would be snack time, then outdoor playtime. I would start fixing dinner. It was like the movie *Groundhog Day*. Everyday felt the same for a while.

Carol

My Two New Besties

Have you heard of personalities that had the sun and the moon? The morning and the night? People who are at the opposite ends of the spectrum, but at the same time have this unexplainable common ground? You can't quite grasp what that common denominator is between them, but it works! And it works so well. That is Jane and Joanie. Side note — the term "bestie" or "BFF" was not created yet, but that's what Jane and Joanie were to me.

Joanie

Joanie has this super engineer-type brain, way out there with physics and math. You've seen those types of people. They put things together and never use the schematic. Every now and then, there's a piece left over. But the object they were putting together works just fine without that one leftover piece. Now, you would think that personality would be very restrictive and calculated, but she's not. Joanie can fly by the seat of her pants better than anybody I know. Joanie looks at something and says, "I can do it better than that. All you need to do is this, this, and this." Bam, it's done! Joanie's son Michael has that gene too. You know the old saying, "Tree to apple."

Joanie could see and do things without batting an eye. Literally. She could do anything she saw. One time, I needed patterns to sew, and I kept getting stuck. Joanie was always there. If the pattern didn't work out right, she snipped and cut and tucked and then it was perfect. As I watched her "fix" what I was doing, I would think, "Oh my gosh... Joanie just cut right into that material without hesitation." It is the same feeling I get now when I press a key on the computer and the whole thing disappears. My heart sinks, but that never seemed to happen to Joanie. The 70's were the years when pinafores were in style for our girls, the Betsy Clark and Holly Hobbie patterns. Joanie made them all with ease. They looked so cute in those outfits.

Joanie's abilities never ceased to amaze me. She and her family belonged to a catamaran sailing club. Almost every weekend, the club went to Mission Bay and sailed their boats. I don't know how Joanie did this, but she quickly became the organizer of their club. They would have very large cookouts on the beach. Joanie would make this gigantic salad! I cannot emphasize enough the size of this salad. She lined a large cooler and filled it with lettuce, tomatoes, carrots, etc. It could probably feed 30-40 people.

She also created all kinds of t-shirts for the group. She knew how to silk screen. She made the regatta trophies out of sand sculpting. I truly don't think there's anything she couldn't do.

Jane

Here we go to the opposite end of the spectrum — Jane. She is meticulous and thrives on the perfection of whatever she is doing. Accuracy is a very important part of Jane's comfort level. When she is working on something, Jane always considers the whole presentation, whether it's wrapping a present or setting the table. She once told me that in her Japanese upbringing, presentation is one of the most important aspects of their culture.

Jane was the one who taught me how to wrap presents. She worked in the gift wrapping department at Buffums (kind of like Macy's). I learned how to make the most beautiful bows from Jane. I learned how to tuck in the edges of the paper and cut the paper just right. I have since tutored my children, nieces, nephews, and grandchildren in the art of present wrapping. Tania has taken over as being the best bow maker in our family! Unfortunately, this wonderful skill isn't really necessary anymore, unless you have a wedding. The premade decorative bags and tissue paper have sent the boxes, wrapping paper, scotch tape, and all that ribbon to the wayside.

The handmade element may be lost, but the importance of presentation still remains, according to Jane. Tania and I were just out there this past spring. We were celebrating several of the ladies' birthdays, all in March. We, of course, have little gifts in bags with tissue paper, no bows. Jane, observing the presentation rule, had to fix the tissue paper. She decided that the tissue paper did not match the bag just right. So she scooted on over there and rearranged it before the guests arrived. That is so like Jane. Gotta love her!

Jane has made probably 1,000 or more origami cranes (birds) for weddings, which bring good luck! She has the patience to make tiny, tedious crafts for celebrations, such as origami boxes for gifts. Jane also quilts beautifully. Another personality trait of Jane's is that she always needed a plan. Every task was always laid out in an orderly fashion with a clear step-by-step progression. Whether we were sewing sequins on Stacy's dance costume or just going to the park, Jane always had a plan.

Jane also showed me the art of the Bento box. She explained that in Japanese culture, parents would make these very fancy lunch boxes for their children called Bento boxes. Every food had its own little section. The food was placed correctly, gently, and attractively in its appropriate section of the box. I had never heard of or seen one before. Another one of the moms on our block was from Okinawa, and she generously gave us a Bento for a going-away present. It is beautifully hand-painted with a lacquered finish. It is still displayed on my bookshelf (minus the food, of course).

The Bento boxes Jane described to me are a far cry from my lunches when I went to school, which consisted of a bologna sandwich with mayonnaise wrapped in wax paper and an apple dropped in a brown paper bag. So after my walk of four blocks, holding tightly to my bag and carrying my books to school, I had a very smashed bologna sandwich in a very crinkled brown bag. I would then fold up the bag after lunch to bring home and use the rest of the week! For you youngsters...that was TRUE RECYCLING!

My two new besties and I grew so close in those short years. Those wonderful ladies welcomed me to Dent Drive with open arms.

Carol

Tea Talk

My adult daughter, Tania, has asked me, "What did you, Jane, and Joanie talk about after we went to school?"

Let me back up a little bit. If you remember, we moved in at the end of September, and Jane and Joanie were so extremely helpful with registering my kids at Gage School. They gave me the address of the school, the phone number of the school, and the principal's name. I had zero experience in transferring my children to a new school, so I still appreciate all that help.

Back to Tania's question. So about a half hour after all the children headed off to school, Jane and Joanie would have coffee. After a few weeks of being in town, I was invited to join the coffee clutch. And, what did we talk about? The same things our adult children talk about now. We talked about our children, our husbands, and trivial things like the price of gas and our electric bills. Just regular moms talking about regular things.

Until one day a few months later. I was hosting coffee at my house. Jane had come over with her coffee cup. All of a sudden, I hear Joanie walking up the sidewalk. She always said, "Knock, knock!" and opened the door. There were two sets of slatted glass windows by my front door. So, of course, you could hear everything on the front porch and the sidewalk.

Joanie comes in with her coffee cup, and she has a friend with her this time. I enjoyed meeting new people, so that was fine with me. This was a lady who didn't live in our neighborhood, and I had never met her before. Joanie introduced her as her friend, Grace, from some place I can't remember. To set the scene, I'm in my kitchen between the stove and the sink underneath the window which faces Jane's house. Joanie, Jane, and Grace are across the counter from me. So there we are, all sitting around, chit-chatting, and drinking our coffee (I was drinking tea, of course).

After some pleasantries and stories, Grace says, "I've got some news. And, I want to share it with you ladies!" Okay, sure. We all like a bit of juicy gossip.

At that moment, Grace pulls up her shirt and says, "I got a boob job a couple of months ago!!" No bra! Just boobs!

I don't really know what I looked like, but I do know what Jane looked like with news like that. Jane's eyes were the size of saucers! The room was quiet, except for Joanie's laugh.

You have to remember it's 1975, and I'm 27 and from the Midwest. Breast implants were just starting to be approved. I had never, ever been around women who had breast implants! And by the look on Jane's face...she hadn't either. Joanie's laughter said she was just as surprised by the 'show and tell' from Grace as we were. Joanie just started laughing out loud, probably from the looks on our faces. I know I didn't say anything, and I don't think Jane said anything either. But Grace...she was very proud of her new boob job. To tell you the truth, I don't really remember how our coffee time ended that day. But I did start to wonder, "What kind of neighborhood did I really move into?" I have to admit that was probably the most interesting coffee talk I ever had in my life!

As a footnote, I never saw Grace again. Also, I don't think I have ever shared this story with Tania. After reading this, I'm guessing she won't ever ask me again what our coffee talks were about.

Tania

Weather Wonder

Being from the Midwest, the beautiful weather in San Diego was both unique and surprising. In fact, living in San Diego meant you didn't experience much weather at all. But there were a couple times per year when you would have some rain. I remember popping open my umbrella and splashing through the puddles outside. It was warm. You could go outside in your raincoat and dance around in the rain because there typically wasn't any thunder or lightning. It was beautiful and carefree.

I do remember one atypical time when we had a thunderstorm while we lived out there. We were standing in our garage with our neighbors, watching the rain come down really, really hard. In San Diego, it was exciting when it rained. All of Dent Drive wanted to see it. It was thundering, and all the native San Diegans were getting a bit nervous and concerned. Coming from the Midwest, we were the weather experts. I remember it beginning to hail, and our neighbors asking if it was snow. We said, "No, this is hail." They weren't sure about the hail (is anyone?). We went on to explain that hail was just little ice balls coming down from the sky. They wanted to run out and touch it (even the adults); it was pretty amazing to them.

I also remember when I experienced my first earthquake. We never had any major earthquakes while we were there, but I do recall hearing and seeing the window glass rattling. I can still see the chandeliers beginning to sway back and forth and the cabinet doors bouncing on their hinges. It was a strange, euphoric sound like a subtle rumbling. It catches you off-guard, and it takes a minute to realize what's happening. At the moment, it feels like it will last forever. Then, it's over as suddenly as it began. It was quite an interesting experience. I don't remember being scared or afraid, but I do remember the almost surreal feeling of experiencing an earthquake firsthand.

Rob

It Takes a Village

My mom and dad were 27 and 28 when we arrived in San Diego. They took quite the risk in leaving their support system and venturing out alone to an unknown city. They did a great job of making our home. Being involved in our school and my little league maintained a constant and continual feeling of comfort and support. I knew we didn't have much money, but it never felt like we were lacking or wanting for anything. We did not take grandiose vacations. In fact, most of our vacations were around Christmas to visit family in St. Louis. My parents hosted many family, friends, and even parents of friends, as many were too intimidated to travel to California by themselves. On weekends, my parents took us out to explore the mountain town of Julian and the vast outdoors of the state parks and beaches. We took trips to Coronado and tours of aircraft carriers. We even experienced the eye-opening education of walking across the border to Tijuana (TJ, as the kids called it back then).

Joanie was California groovy. She was free-spirited and easy-going. She even let her kids call her by her first name, which was a new experience for me. I remember asking my mom if Cyn, Mike, and Holly were her kids. Joanie would walk around barefoot, decked out in a flowing dress or bell bottoms. Of course the sailboats in the front yard only added to the beach aesthetic. Another thing about Joanie was that she really hated it when people would speed through our neighborhood, even to the point where she would yell at cars as they passed by. Her protectiveness, like the other parents, extended beyond her own children and encompassed all of us kids on Dent Drive.

John was a computer science teacher, which I guess explains why they had so many new technologies, like a camera, stereo equipment, and an inground sprinkler system. He was definitely a techie, but he was also one of the funniest people I've ever met. On election night in 1976, he came over to Jane and Sas's house (where we were all hanging out and monitoring the election results), and he had a paper bag filled with peanuts that he handed out to all those in attendance. The election was between Jimmy Carter and Gerald Ford, and I later found out that John handed out peanuts because Carter was a peanut farmer prior to running for president. Joanie and John's house was always full of excitement. It was like a zoo. They had dogs, cats, birds, all kinds of animals running around all the time. Joanie would always rescue any animal that needed saving.

Yonecko was short in stature and spoke English with an Asian accent. Beyond the threats through her louvered windows when we went into her yard, she was happy to take us kids to the movies occasionally. When we went to the movies with Yonecko, she would smuggle in bags of popcorn. She'd pop it all at home, put it in paper grocery bags, and stuff it under her sweater or in a big purse as we walked into the theater. I remember being so nervous and thinking, "I can't believe she is about to sneak in popcorn!" But she always made it in without being noticed. Once we were settled into our seats, she would break out the bag, and we would all share it.

Yonecko's husband, Chris, was the General Manager of a car dealership, so they always had really nice cars. They had a Toyota Celica Supra and a Mercedes Benz. We'd ride in one of those to get to the movies, smuggled popcorn and all.

Jane and Sas were always welcoming to me and my family from day one. They graciously allowed Bret and I to play marathon Monopoly games in their hallway, which was just the beginning of their generosity. Their house was often a gathering place, so it was not unusual to find Joanie, John, my mom, Cyn, Holly, and many others at their house. Jane, as I mentioned, would often provide lunch while I was over there playing. While I do not ever remember either one of them getting upset, Sas was particularly laid back. He practiced Kendo weekly, rode bikes, and hiked. He even had a trademark shake of his head and an, "Oh, geez," which he used to deal with most catastrophes. In addition to Jane's happy disposition and fantastic, unmistakable laugh, I remember my astonishment at how well she used chopsticks to cook. She easily managed to cook bacon and puffy fried rice. They occasionally allowed me to tag along with them and their friends and siblings who played in a tennis league on Friday nights. The highlight was going to the pizza parlor afterwards where Bret and I seemed to get an endless amount of quarters to play pinball.

Billie and Stanley were Steven's parents and were very friendly too. Stanley was handy, and I remember him helping out occasionally with some of our appliances. I believe they owned some rental property, and he took care of the repairs which honed his handyman skillset.

Carol

Machete Mama

Blue Grass doesn't grow in Southern California, just in case you didn't know. No, siree. But ice plants grow and grow and grow. Here's how I would describe my backyard in San Diego: the patio was 10 by 12 feet surrounded by a ribbon of some kind of green stuff they called grass (but I'm not sure what it really was). That ribbon was about 2 feet wide and 30 feet long. Then, there was the hill that went straight up at a plane of 40 degrees at least. It ran parallel to Jackie Drive and was also known as the "Killer Hill." I think the code name "Killer Hill" was justified by the gazillion crashes on bikes, scooters, roller skates, and skateboards. My backyard hill was covered with ice plants. In all honesty, these succulents were necessary to keep the hillside from eroding. Without them, the house at the top of the hill would have been on my patio. At the top of this hill, looking through the fence and out onto the street is where Snowball would sit and watch the world go by.

Let it be known that I did not have the cute tiny, delicate little flowering ice plant. Oh no, that would be too easy to take care of. The owners of the home we rented from just had to plant the super large ice succulent. I had the KING KONG ice plant. Huge and heavy. Very fast growing. It would grow about 2 feet every year. In order to keep the ribbon of grass-like substance intact, I would trim the ice plant back 2 feet annually, just trying to stay ahead of that growth.

Of course, I had never seen or worked with an ice plant before. So, I came to that plant with the average size hand-held, St. Louis-style pruning shears. You guessed it...the average shears didn't do much damage to the ice plant. At this point, I was scouring the garage to find some kind of tool to cut the ginormous plant back. Aha — a machete! Every 28-year-old mom needs a machete in her tool box, right?

The machete turned out to be the perfect tool for the jungle hill. I brought out one 30-gallon trash bag to collect the trimmings from the ice plant. What was I thinking? That stuff was so heavy and so hard to chop. There was no gentle snipping and pruning. I was literally swinging with all my strength, dripping with sweat. I went at it for three hours or more. I must have filled 10 or 12 bags. It was exhausting.

I think Robbie can attest to the difficulty of maintaining the succulent. I may have recruited him once or twice. Moral of the story: If you can't afford a gardener, don't have King Kong succulents on your hill.

Rob

When the Street Lights Come On

The game of choice on Dent Drive was tennis ball, which was played within the confines of the cul-de-sac. The uniforms consisted of gym shorts, tube socks, and, for me, Sears Winner II sneakers. The older kids split a wooden bat in half vertically and would try to hit a tennis ball with the curved side. We'd take white rocks from one of the neighbor's front yard and use them as chalk to mark the bases. We'd try to make even teams, so the older guys would split themselves up between the two teams (Scott was the only one who could hit the ball all the way from home plate to Jackie Drive. Us younger kids were awestruck by that). Then, we'd break into positions: pitcher, shortstop, and outfielder. The team batting provided the catcher. The streets of Tuxford and Dent formed a "Y" at the cul-de-sac where Jeff and Laurie's house was. Dent was the only street in fair territory, so you had to hit it left of second base or it was foul.

There were very few rules — you could catch the ball off a roof for an out, and you were out if the ball was caught or if the ball made it back to the pitcher before you made it to first base. You did have to be careful if you hit the ball into Yonecko's yard. If you hit the ball into her yard, she'd yell from her window, "Get outta my yard! I'll break your legs!" when you tried to retrieve it. This was especially funny because her sons played with us too, and they weren't immune to her threats either.

We'd play tennis ball from eight in the morning until dinnertime. Sometimes we would take a lunch break; sometimes we wouldn't. No one ever wanted to leave when we heard our moms calling us in for dinner, but the game would pick up the next day. It was critical that the person storing the equipment would not go on vacation or have plans without turning the bat and ball over to someone else.

We also played a lot of football, especially when winter came around. Most days we would play on the long stretch of street in the neighborhood from the cul-de-sac to Jackie. We'd play two-on-two or three-on-three depending on who showed up that day. Whenever we were in the huddle, whoever was playing quarterback would draw the route you were supposed to run on your shirt. Most of the routes would be something like run to the neighbor's car, over towards Simba, curl back, then catch the ball.

A few times we walked up to Grossmont Community College and played touch football on their field. We felt like a big deal playing on a college field. Grossmont had a vending machine that sold pencils with NFL team logos on them. We spent our quarters trying to get our favorite teams, which was ultimately a waste because it was random. Nobody wanted the Tampa Bay Buccaneers. I always wanted the Cardinals or Chargers. I bet I still have some of those pencils lying around somewhere.

Ditch 'em was another popular game on Dent Drive. Ditch 'em was basically like hide-and-go-seek outside after dark. You had to stay within predetermined boundaries, but no spots were off limits within that area. We hid in bushes, behind cars in driveways, anywhere we thought we wouldn't be found. When cars would drive by, we would try our best to avoid the shine (and inevitable discovery) of the headlights. There were also plenty of games of HORSE and Cops and Robbers.

Carol

It Never Rains in Southern California

Have you ever heard that song by Albert Hammond that goes, "It never rains in Southern California. But man, it pours!"? Well you can ask Jane if that's true. Her backyard turned into a floodplain when it rained, putting her patio underwater. And, Jane's favorite words were, "Eww, yuck!" But never fear, the Dent boys were there. They had their shovels in hand and were ready to dig the famous canal between Jane's home and mine. The canal was the design of our local engineer, Joanie, and the labor was provided by the Dent Drive Gang, our boys. The canal started at the back patio and went all the way to the street. It was at least 30 feet long and 8 inches wide and made of hard sand that felt like concrete. Robbie and Bret dug all day long! We still have conversations about the canal 45 years later. They got the work done, and it didn't stop them from their evening tennis ball game.

Warm Rain

There was another time when it was raining pretty hard. San Diego streets are not set up very well for downpours. Robbie, Tania, and I were watching the rain from our kitchen windows.

We lived on the corner of Jackie Drive (the extremely steep hill) and Dent Drive. The water came down Jackie, swirling with volume. There was no thunder or lightning. In St. Louis, if there is no thunder or lightning, then there are no restrictions. The kids were just chomping at the bit to go out in the street and slosh around in the puddles. They pleaded, "Gosh. Can we go out, mom?" It had been raining for a few hours, so eventually I relented.

They dashed out — no shoes, no sandals, just bare feet. They were jumping and kicking at the fast-flowing water in the street. With rain pouring down, both of them looked like the orphans that just came off the set of *Les Miserables*. The giggling and belly laughs were well worth the mess. The new neighborhood probably thought we were crazy. Sometimes being crazy can be fun.

Tania

Going to School

When I arrived in San Diego, I was five years old. I had no idea what life as a student was going to be like. I had only been in school in St. Louis for a month or so when we moved. Frankly, I don't even remember it. I do, however, remember going to Gage Elementary in San Diego. I was in kindergarten, and Robbie was in third grade.

We walked to school each day as a large group of kids. For some reason, we all ended up at our house before heading up to school. The neighbors didn't knock on the door and wait to be let in; they knocked on the doors and then let themselves in. Kids walked into each other's houses all the time. Our house quickly became the gathering spot.

While waiting to go to school, we would all be sitting in the family room watching the *Electric Company* on TV. I loved that show, especially when they would break the words into syllables. There were two faces on the screen and each one would say a syllable (B…. oat…boat). The letters would come out of their mouths. As a child, it was so cool to see the letters flying across the TV screen!

My brother and his friends would be sitting in the family room too, talking about whatever boys talk about. Most days Bret was his usual silly self. He'd be coming up with new languages and using phrases like, "That's so rad." Other days, Bret would be running late. He and his mom would have gotten into an argument, and he would be grumpy. Or, if he had a poor night's sleep, he would come over with his hair sticking up on one side of his head. My mom would say, "Uh oh, Bret has horns today. It's gonna be a rough day for him." On those days, he wasn't his usual silly self.

His sister, Stacy, would come over too. She would stand in front of the TV, dazed and mesmerized by whatever show was on. She always carried her bed pillow folded over one of her arms and had her index finger in her mouth. Then, my mom would come in, tell us to turn off the TV, and rush us off to school. We walked to school; it was a one mile walk. Not many kids can say they do that these days. Now remember, I was in kindergarten. Back in the 70's, kindergarten was a half-day program. At five or six years old, I would walk home alone at lunch time. At this time, my mom was not working, so she was home when I got there.

When I would arrive home, my mom and I would eat lunch together. Just the two of us. It was a precious time in my life. I mean, who doesn't want time alone with their mom? Our kitchen had a breakfast bar with olive green countertops...groovy! One side of the counter had four black vinyl bar stools. The kitchen side of the counter had a pull-out cutting board. My mom always ate her lunch from the cutting board, and I always sat across from her on one of the bar stools. Lunch was simple: tomato soup and grilled cheese. The memory is so warm and comforting.

When Stacy started school, she would walk to school with us too. There were times when Stacy was so focused on the TV that we would all leave for school, and she would be left standing there mesmerized. My mom must have been cleaning up the kitchen when she noticed her. She'd yell, "Stacy! They left without you!" Stacy would run out the door and, eventually, catch up with us. I was always near the back of the pack, being a girl and one of the youngest children. My brother and his friends were always ahead of us. There were two routes we could take to and from school. We could go up Jackie Drive or up Highwood Drive. Stacy and I would walk home from school together, and we would decide which way to go. I think we mostly walked home on Jackie, so we could pick flowers for our moms and play with the foxtails in people's yards. We would pull the fluffy seeds from the bottom of the stalk to the top and throw the seeds in the air, kind of like blowing dandelions. I'm sure we were imagining throwing fairy dust into the air.

One day on our way home from school, Stacy and I stopped to pet a dog through the fence of someone's yard. It was a cute white, fluffy dog. After a while, I guess I felt like it was time to head on home, so I left Stacy. I'm sure I told her I was going to leave, but she just kept on petting the dog. I arrived home, went into my house, and did whatever kids did after school. I remember Jane walking in the house looking for Stacy. I told her she didn't come home with me because she stayed to pet the dog. Jane got in her car and drove up Jackie Drive. There was Stacy still petting and playing with that little, white dog. She has always been a fun-loving person. Imagine not having a worry in the world. Imagine the childlike innocence of just sitting and playing with a dog. Those were the days.

Gage Elementary was so different from schools in the Midwest. Back in the day, it had an outdoor, open-air feel to it. When I returned to visit my old school, it still had classrooms that led to the exterior grounds. Unfortunately, the school was now surrounded by chain-link fences to keep kids in and intruders out. Now, it sort of has the appearance of a prison. But back in the day, it felt sunny and free.

One of the things I loved most when I was a student there was eating my lunch outside. The cafeteria had outside lunch tables, and I remember choosing one of those tables almost everyday. I absolutely loved that warm sunshine and fresh air. Every single classroom door opened to the outdoors. It was an incredible feeling — stepping out of a classroom into the warm air. Since I had been away, they had painted some murals on the exterior walls to make the school more appealing. Being there brought back a lot of happy memories.

Rob

Lyman Judson Gage

Every morning, Bret and Stacy would meet up with Tania and I at our house before school. We would all make the mile-long trek together to Lyman Judson "Gage" Elementary School. There was no grass in the schoolyard, only sand. My fifth and sixth grade classes were held in trailers because the school was overcrowded, so the upper grades had to be moved out of the permanent facility. Of course, there was no air conditioning, so those trailers got scorching hot when the Santa Ana Winds blew in off the desert. A couple of times we were sent home early because it was over a hundred degrees outside and, most likely, inside the trailers.

A favorite teacher of mine was Mr. G. in fifth grade. I remember he would always read to us for 15 minutes after lunch and recess to regain our focus. As an adult, I still think back and wonder how he made it through *Old Yeller*. I remember him using the Padres players' batting averages to help us learn division. We were all assigned a player to follow and calculate their batting average throughout the season. Mine was Gene Tenace.

Living in San Diego, we often ate our school lunch outside on picnic tables. We'd go into the cafeteria, grab our lunches, and head back out to the outdoor lunch tables. Even though I brought my lunch from home most of the time, I still remember the cafeteria's burgers (which had to be made out of soybean or something because they tasted and smelled so funny) and the notorious bowl of chili and peanut butter sandwich combo. My mom would often make my lunch, which consisted of a sandwich, cut carrots or celery, and a plastic baggie of chips. The best days were when there was a surprise Ding Dong, Hostess cupcake, or container of crackers with processed cheese and the little red stick to be used as a spreader (one of my all-time favorites) showed up. My mom frequently put little notes in my lunch too. I was careful to read them inside the bag so that others would not see them. Like most elementary schoolers, we would occasionally trade snacks. Carrots and celery did not garner much leverage in the craft.

Pizza Hut was the lunch of choice when we had half days (which were every other Wednesday). Because my mom and Bret's mom both worked as teacher's assistants at the school, we would all go out to lunch together. Bret and I would compete to see how many pieces of pizza we could eat from the buffet (after starting with a salad covered in creamy Italian dressing). I distinctly remember eating seven pieces of pizza on at least one occasion. While I think both of us hit that high water mark, I don't think either one of us ever made it past that. Remarkably, I don't think that ever affected our ability to play outside in the afternoon. Seven pieces of pizza and we were ready to go!

Tania

Stranger Danger

In the 70's, no one was really worried about their kids being taken. We walked to and from school alone — a mile each way. I'm sure there were abductions, but no one really worried. At least, my mom didn't. I knew I shouldn't talk to strangers. But, what is a stranger? One time at school, a staff member told me to meet my mom on the opposite side of the playground because she was supposed to pick me up there. I remember standing alone along a long chain-link fence. I was probably in first or second grade, and I was by myself. My mom wasn't there to pick me up. To make things worse, it was raining that day. So, I was standing on the sidewalk under my umbrella waiting, but she still wasn't there. My heart was pounding, and I was getting worried.

Then, a man in his car pulled up and said, "Hi, I'm Mr. So-And-So, and your mom sent me to come pick you up. Her car broke down and won't start." My mom sent a stranger to pick me up. Yes — a person I didn't know at all drove up to school and picked me up. My gut instinct said, "You're not supposed to go. You're not supposed to get in that car." But then why would my mom send somebody else? I was looking around to see if anyone was going to acknowledge my predicament. Was anyone going to stop me? Mr. So-And-So reiterated that it was okay and to get in the car. So guess what? I got in the car! Completely devastating, right? I was scared, and I could feel it in the pit of my stomach. In the moment, I knew I shouldn't have done it, but I did it anyway. He drove me home, and I ran as fast as I could into my house.

Well — it turned out that my mom's car really did break down. She really did send somebody to come pick me up, and it all turned out okay. I was reunited with my mother and all was well, but could you imagine sending a stranger to pick up your child nowadays? Talk about stranger danger.

Carol

The Last Stop

There was one constant on Dent Drive: I was always the last stop before all the kids went to school. I still remember how much energy was in my house on those mornings. Oh my gosh, the chitter-chatter was amazing. You could hear it buzzing above the cartoons blaring in the background.

My mantra was the same every morning.
> *Do you have your homework?*
> *Do you have your books?*
> *Do you have your lunches?*
> *You guys, you're going to be late!*

And, last but not least...
> *Put that down! You can play with that when you get home.*

After that, they'd all pack up and scurry out the door.

One time after the kids left, I was walking past the kitchen table and looked to my right to turn off the TV. I did a double take and there sat Stacy. She was sitting on her bottom with her knees under her chin and her finger in her mouth. She had absolutely no idea that everybody had left. She was mesmerized by the television. I went over to her and said, "Stacy, everybody left. You're going to be so late for school. Get going!" With that, she looked at me and then around at the vacant room. She stood up still confused and dazed, as her eyes went big and round. It was finally registering. You could see the wheels turn, and as greased lightning, she ran out the door.

Tania

Peaches and Pizza

Traditions are sometimes created without even trying. When I was in elementary school, my mom and Jane both worked as teacher's assistants at Gage. On Wednesdays, we would get out of school early, and our moms would take us out to lunch. I'm not really sure how often this happened, but I do remember it occurring on multiple occasions. Jane, Stacy, Bret, my mom, Robbie, and I would go to one of our two favorite spots: Pizza Hut and Peach Blossom. My mom jokes that she probably spent her entire week's paycheck just taking us out to lunch on those days. But it was worth it; the memories we made were priceless.

Pizza Hut was one of my favorite restaurants because they had a two-seater corner booth. Stacy and I would get our own personal pizza and sit in that little corner booth together. We felt like we were grown-ups. Little did we know, our moms probably enjoyed the fact that we weren't near them so they were able to do all of their gossiping without us around. We would jump up from the booth and go ask our moms how much longer we were going to be there. They'd just shoo us away. We would run back and giggle because we were excited they weren't ready to leave yet.

I remember my mom teaching Stacy how to dip her pizza crust in salt, which made it taste just like a pretzel. It's funny how those memories come back to me every time I eat pizza. To this day, I still dip my crust in salt.

Egg Drop Soup and Finger Bowls

Sometimes we would go to Peach Blossom, which was a Chinese restaurant. Stacy and I would get in trouble for eating our egg drop soup off our spoons backwards. We did it anyway and giggled the entire time.

Peach Blossom also gave you bowls (complete with a slice of lemon) to wash your fingers before the meal. We spent more time playing in the finger bowls than we did eating. Our hands were mighty clean for our meal.

Tania

Teachers: My First Impressions

I started kindergarten in San Diego at Gage Elementary. I had some pretty interesting times there. Needless to say, my crazy school experiences definitely played into my desire to become a teacher.

Mrs. Witchy and the Trash Can

When I enrolled in kindergarten, I was in Mrs. Witchy's class (Mrs. Witchy was not her real name. In fact, all of the teachers' names have been changed to ensure anonymity). She was about 100 years old, very skinny, and had a large beehive hairstyle. The best way to describe her is that she reminded me of Dolly Parton. Back in those days, rules and disciplinary measures were pretty lenient. But there came a time when I'm certain that she was completely fed up with a particular student in my class. So she took matters into her own hands. She literally put him in a trash can to control his behavior. It was a large, black brute trash can...not a kitchen size one. I have no idea what the child did to get himself into such a predicament; all I know is that he ended up in a trash can. Even as a young child, this type of discipline sent me into a tizzy. I began to have stomach aches and nightmares. One night my mom even found me in the corner of my room screaming because I had a dream about the teacher putting me in a trash can. After that incident, my mom went to the principal and had me removed from Mrs. Witchy's classroom. I remember walking into the principal's office and finding my mom there. My mom raised us with the guiding phrase of, "Stick it out," which meant, "Just deal with it." That's what we did most of the time but not in this instance. Seeing her there proved how impactful of an experience that was for me.

Things got better. My second kindergarten teacher was much nicer, and I flourished. In my new classroom, I remember painting being one of my favorite things to do. We had this giant easel in the classroom and were able to take turns painting. I absolutely loved it. I also vividly remember learning how to read. I can still see the Dick and Jane books set up on the easel. I remember the thrill and excitement I felt as I was reading about Dick and Jane. I even remember the moment when it all clicked, and I realized I was actually reading. Once you begin to read, your whole world opens up before you. Then, you start reading street signs, newspapers, cereal boxes, anything you can get your hands on. You find words that you recognize. It was an exciting time for me. I was a reader!

Another Unpleasant Teacher

By the time I was in second grade, my mom was working as a teacher's aide in a first grade classroom at Gage. In fact, my mom and Jane both worked at the school part-time. Jane was a teacher's assistant in a third grade classroom. They would send us off to walk to school like usual, then they would arrive to work closer to when school started. I'm pretty sure that was just to get us out of their hair for a few minutes of peace and quiet.

My second grade experience was horrible. I had Mrs. Meanie, who was one of the meanest teachers I recall ever having. I don't know if it was because she was so close to retirement, had the shortest fuse, or the worst temperament ever, but I did know that she yelled a lot and flew off the handle quite often. I was so afraid in that classroom that I would sneak out and down the hall to the classroom my mother was working in. She would be sitting at the desk, and I would just appear, standing right next to her. She would jump and yell, "Oh my gosh, Tania! What are you doing here?"

I would say, "I'm scared. I don't want to be in that classroom. That teacher is mean."

She would whisper, "You can't keep running out of class. You have to get back in there."

So she would walk me back to class, and we would wait outside the room. She'd then shoo me in when Mrs. Meanie wasn't looking. Needless to say, the teacher never noticed I was gone (which says quite a bit about her teaching abilities). Since my mom already got me out of my kindergarten classroom, she knew she probably couldn't make the same request again. That opportunity had been taken, so I stuck it out.

One time, a student I didn't know very well was having some trouble staying in his seat. So Mrs. Meanie decided to take the boy's chair and put it on top of his desk. She picked the boy up, put him in the chair atop the desk, and wrapped masking tape around his legs and the chair to secure him in place. Then, she taped his ankles and his hands down too. I think my eyeballs got as big as silver dollars, and my jaw dropped to the floor. I panicked, so I ran out of the room to tell my mother. How long that child sat taped to his chair on top of his desk is a wonder to me to this day. Looking back (and from the perspective of an educator), I wonder if the child told his parents what happened. Did the parents contact the school? Did the teacher get reprimanded? What a horrible experience for that child and for the other kiddos watching it happen. I think about that a lot.

Another time in second grade, we were sitting on the floor learning multiplication tables (back when memorization was a skill we had to master). The boy next to me was running his pencil all over the tile floor, back and forth in a crescent shape. Kind of like he was daydreaming. I remember Mrs. Meanie turning around from the chalkboard. Then, she saw the pencil marks all over the floor. I didn't even have my pencil with me, but she screamed and scolded both of us. I was too scared to say anything! She might tape me to a chair, and I was not near the door so I couldn't escape to my mom. I was stuck! We had to spend our recess time cleaning up the marks with erasers. Now back in the 70's, I guess we didn't rat on each other too often because I don't think my mom ever told anyone in administration what happened in that classroom. Mrs. Meanie was the worst-tempered teacher I ever had. But, I persevered and made it out alive. She taught me exactly how NOT to treat others.

Peanut Butter Waffles

In third grade, I was blessed with an amazing teacher, Mrs. Y. I remember wanting to be in her class so badly. Teachers' reputations really get around, and I knew from what I heard that I would love having her as a teacher. I secretly hoped and prayed to be in her class. This was also the same classroom that Jane worked in each day. My mom told me I would have to call Jane by her last name if I was going to be in that classroom. Having Jane in my third grade class was an added safety net for me, and I was perfectly fine with that.

Mrs. Y. had a great reputation for loving what she did and caring for her students as people. I remember her smile and her laugh. She truly enjoyed teaching. You could see it in her face. The activities we did were fun and enjoyable in the eyes of a third grader. Mrs. Y. was famous for having a day of the week where she would cook and make the class something with peanut butter in it (remember, this was the 70's, so there weren't really any restrictions or concerns about food allergies). She must have absolutely loved peanut butter because I think everything she cooked included that secret ingredient. Or at least that's what I remember. Maybe this was all she knew how to cook! I didn't care; it was fun! She was the person who taught me to put peanut butter on waffles (topped with a generous drizzle of syrup), and they were absolutely delicious. If you haven't tried peanut butter waffles, I highly recommend them. Mrs. Y. would use a griddle to make our food, and she even set up a station to show us step-by-step directions for the recipe. It was like being on the set of a cooking show. Maybe that was the start of my love of cooking.

A Wonderful Year

I also remember having my first crush that year. He was a cute boy named Chris, who was blonde and quiet. We sat next to each other and passed notes back and forth. I also found comfort in knowing that Jane was in my classroom, so this was the best year of my whole educational career in San Diego. I had Jane (and my first crush) in my classroom. Mrs. Y. was my teacher. We were cooking and making stained glass crafts out of tissue paper. It was such a refreshing time.

Rob

"We Killed Two Cans!"

San Diego holds a lot of great food memories for me. Back in those days, food was still very regionalized. There were very few Mexican restaurants in the Midwest. I don't think Taco Bell had arrived in St. Louis yet, but they were definitely in San Diego. McDonald's was probably the most national chain. There was one right by our house. They first introduced their breakfast menu in the 70's, with the Egg McMuffin, on which I would put grape jelly. An instant classic.

Not only during the school year, but also in the summer, most meals were at home. Our moms would make us lunch. I remember Jane making Bret and I the classic lunch of hard salami and American Cheese sandwiches and Campbell's Condensed Beef Noodle soup. I'd always request ketchup on my sandwiches (which sounds terrible now and did then to Jane), and Bret would always excitedly exclaim, "We killed two cans!" after we finished lunch.

My mom would make us what I now call the precursor to nachos. Doritos were relatively new, and nachos were the newest food trend taking Southern California by storm (or at least they were new to us). My mom would take a jar of Cheez Whiz, which was glass, and heat it up in a pot of boiling water. She'd then take the melted cheese and drizzle it over Doritos. And there you have it — homemade nachos!

Sweet Tooth

Bret and I, and many on Dent Drive, had to try Pop-Rocks. What an interesting and scary sensation. At the time, there was much discussion about the dangers of Pop-Rocks and how they could explode in your mouth if you put a whole package in at one time. That never happened to us. While sweets were not my typical go-to snack, I did like Marathon Bars back in those days. These were about the size of a beef jerky stick but were chocolate-covered caramel twists shaped like a pretzel. Meanwhile, Tania and Stacy ate (and pretended to smoke) their candy cigarettes. Bret and Stacy, along with Jane, introduced us to the coolest Japanese candy which had edible wrappers! The wrappers would melt away in your mouth as you chewed.

We went out as a group on Halloween, and I remember one house on our route that typically handed out Ding Dongs instead of candy. That was a house you did not want to miss each year!

Carol

No Midwestern Cuisine

Before moving to San Diego, my traveling circumference was probably 100 miles. Things don't change a lot in 100 miles. But in 1975, I found myself 1,792 miles from St. Louis and things were a little different. Actually things were a lot different.

Prior to living in San Diego, my only experience with tacos were the ones from Jack in the Box at the low price of 1 jumbo taco for 25¢. The food connoisseur that I am now blossomed because of the enrichment from four years on Dent Drive. Jane made tacos on the stove in her kitchen. She would cook the corn tortillas in oil and fill them with meat and toppings. They were amazing. But even better than Jane's tacos were her mother's shredded beef burritos. She would make them for us every time we went back to visit our Dent Drive Gang over the years. Such a treat!

There was also a definite staple at every meal at Jane's home — steamed rice. Yep, even if you were having mashed potatoes, you would have steamed rice too. Spaghetti? Yep, steamed rice was right next to it.

Tea Time at Jane's

One time at Jane's, she offered me a cup of tea. I accepted and she poured something yellow into a cup with no handles. I looked at it thinking, "What am I gonna do with this yellow water?" So, I asked her, "What is this?" She said, "It's green tea. It's very healthy for you." So I said, "If it's GREEN tea, why is it yellow?" Jane just started laughing. At the time, the only tea I was familiar with was black Lipton tea. I became quite the connoisseur of green tea after all the lunches we had at the little Chinese restaurant called Peach Blossom. So many wonderful memories were made over tea.

Joanie's Concoctions

There was one time that I walked into Joanie's house (using our secret code of knock, knock, knock, and enter), and she was back in the kitchen putting a squid in a pot of boiling water. I was looking at this gray squid with tentacles and suckers, wondering just how they were going to eat it. Joanie was just talking away. I couldn't tell you what was said because I was so fixated on that big boiling pot with tentacles flopping around. I think I just went home and had a cup of tea instead of staying for lunch that day.

Tania

"God Made You Washable"

One of the coolest things about my mom was that she had several catchphrases worth repeating. One of them was, "God made you washable." When she would say that to us, it meant, "Please go on out and play in the dirt. Make mud pies. Pick up bugs. Have a good time. Be kids." Dirt-encrusted fingernails and mud-stained clothes didn't matter because you know, "God made you washable."

Hit the Road

My mom also had some phrases she used when she wanted us to get out of the house. She would tell us to, "Hit the road," or, "Go play in traffic." To this day, Stacy still thinks it's hilarious that Carol would tell us to go "hit the road." I remember the day that Stacy actually said, "Okay! Let's go hit the road!" Then, she walked outside and started hitting the road with her fist. We rolled around laughing as hard as we could.

Blow the Stink Off You

My mom got this one from her mom. She'd say, "Go outside and blow the stink off you." When you break that sentence down, it doesn't make a good impression and doesn't make much sense. It's actually kind of gross. Who says that to their kids? But in essence, it meant GO OUTSIDE. And we did — every chance we got!

Carol

Fitness Goals, Stained Glass, and Tennis

My besties and I tried out quite a few new things together in San Diego. They encouraged me to try many things I wouldn't have done on my own. That's what besties are for, right?

Fitness Goals

One day, Joanie came up with the grand idea that we should get in tip-top shape for the summer. Ugh! She found a lady who was leading exercise classes at a park. That was actually a great idea because we could bring our children. They could play on the playground within our vision, and we could exercise with the trainer. So we were doing all these calisthenics when our trainer decided that we needed to run a mile. I don't think I ever ran a mile in my whole life before that (or after, for that matter). I know that I looked over at Jane and Joanie with an expression of, "ARE YOU CRAZY?" We're just going to pop up and run a mile? I'm absolutely positive that we never broke any world records, but I do remember being very proud of myself. The instructor clocked me at 11 minutes, which I thought was wonderful and is my personal best to this day.

After class, Jane was talking to the personal trainer. The trainer suggested this great powder (which was full of vitamins and proteins, according to the trainer) you mix with water. So Jane bought this miracle powder. The next morning, she brought a glass over and said, "Carol, try this. It's gonna be so good for you. It'll give you energy and everything!" I looked at the glass. It didn't look very attractive. It had a kind of clay color and was lumpy. I thought, "Okay. I'm going to get in shape, so I'll try it." I took a big swig and had to spit it out. Jane stood there laughing. I said, "Jane, were you trying to poison me? That was disgustingly gross!" She couldn't even answer because she was laughing so hard. There went $30 down the tubes, or should I say the kitchen sink. Thus marked the end of our fitness careers.

Stained Glass

But, of course, we had other great and exciting things to try. Joanie came up with another brilliant idea! She thought we needed to take a stained glass course at the junior college. I honestly have to say I thoroughly enjoyed this class. I definitely lack artistic ability, but I thrive on socialization! I felt creative even though I wasn't. Jane, Joanie, and I had a corner spot in the back of the classroom. We would talk in very low voices (yeah, right). And sometimes, we would giggle while the teacher was trying to explain how to solder the lead around these beautiful stained glass pieces. He thought I was the instigator. Out of nowhere, he hurled an eraser at our table. Jane and Joanie threw me under the bus. They looked at me like I was the distraction, so they wouldn't get in trouble. Now this time, Joanie was the one bent over laughing uncontrollably. Sounds like the guilty party was doing all the laughing, if you ask me.

Tennis, Anyone?

At one point, I had mentioned to Jane that I would like to play tennis, but I didn't know how. She said she was going to take some lessons on Saturday mornings and asked if I would like to join. I said, "Yes, of course." I proceeded to go to Fed Mart (predecessor to Walmart) and purchased a brand new tennis racket. No, I did not know anything about buying a tennis racket. All I knew was that it was the most affordable one.

Saturday morning came and I hopped in the car with Jane. I entered the tennis court with my brand new tennis racket in hand. We met the instructor with several other people. The instructor asked me, "Are you right-handed or left-handed when playing tennis?" I looked at him wide-eyed and said, "I don't know," as I put the tennis racket in my left hand, tossed it to my right hand, and then back again. I scrunched my shoulders and said, "I really don't know." He looked at me and said, "Put the racket down on the ground." So I did. I thought I was in trouble before I even started lessons. He then told me to pick up the racket. So I picked the racket up with my right hand and he said, "You're right-handed in tennis." That was interesting to me because I always considered myself left-handed. It was at that time I realized that I only eat and write with my left hand. I do all athletic activities with my right hand, including throwing, batting, catching, and playing racquetball and tennis. This was an epiphany hitting me at 29 years old. We ended up having a lot of fun, even though I didn't play very well.

The Three Besties

After hearing about Jane and Joanie, you may ask yourself what part of the triangle is Carol? I've been thinking about it for quite some time, and I decided I am the obtuse one. A little bit over 90 degrees but not quite 180 degrees. Jane and Joanie encouraged me to do so many things in those four short years that I never would've tried on my own. I'm immensely grateful for all the experiences I shared with these two wonderful ladies.

Rob

Beach Bums

When your neighbors have boats in their front yard, you know you're in California. The family across the street had two catamarans in their yard: Simba the Prindle and the Hobie Cat. All three of their kids were great at sailing. Mike, who looked like a prototypical soccer player, would occasionally take us all out on Mission Bay. We would sail a lot faster than we even thought was possible. He was typically wearing board shorts and no shirt all year long. Along with his sisters, Cyn and Holly, he would strap himself to the mast, then swing out over the ocean. They were all great sailors who were absolutely fearless.

A few more of our beach activities were body surfing and boogie boarding. We had the K-Mart boogie board, which was basically just a piece of styrofoam. But it worked. We would ride the waves and have loads of fun for hours. Memories of beach days with friends are full of fun times, seagulls trying to steal your food, and getting sand in your sandwiches and on every square inch of your body. It's funny that the water didn't feel cold as a kid. Never a complaint!

Tania

All Things Beachy

John and Joanie, our neighbors across the street, had sailboats and were true beach-loving people. I considered Michael, their son, to be an avid sailor. He seemed to have this confidence about him. He was always enthusiastic when it came to sailing. He would encourage you to go for a sailboat ride with a, "Come on, let's go! Let's get out on the water. It's great. It's going to be fun!"

We would go to the beach with their family and have picnics together. We would sit in the sand and play in the ocean. It was such fun learning to ride our boogie boards and letting the waves take us onto the beach. We would each take turns going out on the sailboat with Mike. He just seemed to be so fearless out on the water. We would be riding along, and he'd change the direction of the sail. Then, the sailboat would lean to one side and you'd be way high up sitting on one pontoon. Then, it would tip back down as he would change the sail to another direction, and you would sail along with the water churning underneath the mesh. I remember truly enjoying it and feeling like it was one of the coolest things I've ever experienced. Because of those incredible moments, I have such an urge to get back to the beach every year. It just brings back so many wonderful memories of unforgettable times with great people.

Sometimes we would have bonfires at night. We would sit out on the beach around a fire, watching the waves crash against the shore. Our skin felt salty and a little bit sunburned (since none of us ever used any sunscreen), but we were happy as can be.

Rob

Mind-Blowing Technology

The first time I saw a microwave was in San Diego. Jane and Sas were the first ones on Dent Drive to own one. There were no special settings or buttons; there was just a simple dial with a timer. At the time, we thought it was so fancy. I remember my mom taking frozen meat over to Jane's house and popping it into the microwave to thaw it out for dinner.

Another piece of mind-blowing technology was Joanie and John's inground sprinkler system. Now that was something else I had never seen before — I thought it was so cool and high tech. It's almost like Dent Drive was ahead of its time.

Pong and Atari (Asteroids, Defender, and Tank Battle were all favorites of mine) were new on the scene, and we marveled at how we could hook up this box to our TV and play games. Dent Drive was wired for cable TV when we moved in — something else that was different from our St. Louis home. Home Box Office (which later became HBO) would run movies from late afternoon to early morning. It was something like 8 or 9 hours of programming.

Carol

Our First Christmas in San Diego

One afternoon, I was going to the Fletcher Parkway Mall. Remember there was no GPS back then, so I would ask the neighbors how to get somewhere, write down the street names, turns, and iconic landmarks, and off I went. It usually went something like, "Go down Jackie, take a right on Lake Murray, and a left on Navajo by Great Western Bank." In this way, I made it to the mall. As I entered the large indoor area, I really had to do a double take. Being the world traveler that I was all the way from St Louis to San Diego, I was taken aback by the inconsistencies of decorating for Christmas! There were no Evergreen Christmas trees! They put lights on their palm trees for Christmas! What the heck? Who ever heard of that? How dumb. To have a real Christmas, you have to have Evergreen trees with lights on them.

Anyway, all the way through the mall, palm trees were decorated with white lights. I couldn't wait to get back home to tell the family about this discovery over dinner! This was going to be a great story to tell the parents in St. Louis on this weekend's phone call too.

My mom flew out the first week in December for a short visit, even though she was terrified of flying. I had to hand it to her because I know that took courage. I guess you would call her the Ambassador for both sides of the family. I'm sure she was tasked with reporting back to the whole family that we actually lived in a home, in a nice neighborhood, with food on the table. She just wanted to make sure of everything. Robbie and Tania had so much fun with their grandma in town. She loved and adored them so much.

Now that I'm a grandma, I realize how I must have ripped their hearts out by relocating their grandchildren 1,792 miles away. The grandchildren they saw twice a week. The grandchildren they took on vacations to the Ozarks. Their whole world, the center of their universe left them in September, as they stood in the driveway of our old home, sadly waving goodbye.

Surprise Gift

After grandma went back to St. Louis, we all fell back into our routines. The kids had school. I had a new job and was now being invited to have coffee (tea for me) with Jane and Joanie, after the kids went off to school each morning. Bob rode to work with two other guys everyday, so I could keep our car for the kids and errands. One day, one of Bob's coworkers wanted to stop at a pet store on their way home. He and his wife were buying a Dachshund for their children as a surprise for Christmas. While there, Bob found the cutest small, all white puppy. We discussed how that would help with the transition of our first "alone" Christmas. The kids would be so busy with the new puppy they wouldn't have time to be too sad. So on his way home the following evening, he bought the pup but had the store owner hold onto it until closer to Christmas.

It was Christmas Eve and when Bob was dropped off that day, he quietly lifted the garage door just a crack and slipped the little pup in. We figured the puppy would wander around in there for a little while, then start to whine. Bob came in the front door and looked at me, giving a thumbs up. The Christmas package had arrived. All was working out well. I had the table set in the kitchen area right next to the garage. We were eating dinner, but there were no sounds coming from the garage. No scratching or barking. No whining. Of course, nothing. It's Murphy's law. I said, "My goodness, I know I hear something in the garage. It sounds like some kind of animal got in there." The kids looked back and forth from Bob to me. Still no noise in the garage or any movement from the table.

Bob instructed that they better get out there and find out what that sound was! Bob and I started doing the dishes and clearing off the table, smiling to ourselves and each other. We could hardly contain our personal and parental excitement. We wanted that surprise so much! The kids went out into the garage, and we heard a small amount of rumbling around. No big squeal of joy for a couple of minutes. How long could it possibly take for them to find a white puppy in a dark garage? We kept looking at each other and waiting. Finally, Tania screams, "A puppy is in here!"

She came through the doorway with the white puppy on her shoulder like she used to carry her Rub-A-Dub baby doll. Robbie was glued to her side. He was grinning from ear to ear and reaching around to have his turn at holding the puppy. Those two had the biggest smiles on their little faces! I cried. I was overjoyed that they were so happy. Nothing in the whole world makes a mom happier and makes her heart swell more than to see her children happy! I mean that genuine smile with all their teeth showing, not the polite smile. The happiness that comes from the inside.

Attached to the pup's collar, Bob had the owner of the pet store write a little note that said, "To Robbie and Tania. Take care of me. Love, Santa."

Amazing Abilities

We named him Snowball. Quite appropriate, don't you think? We Barrales were so creative! And to make a long story short, we found out Snowball was deaf. I was told by the vet that it is not uncommon for albino dogs to be deaf. At first, I was a little sad, and I was hoping that would not affect the kids' relationship with their gift from Santa. Of course, it didn't. If anything, the empathy for their deaf puppy made them love him even more, if that was possible. Snowball never exceeded a maximum of 14 pounds with his white fur and blue eyes. Snowball really never barked.

We taught Snowball to obey commands by using hand signals. How did we do that? Well, we took what we had learned from the trainers at SeaWorld, who trained the animals to obey hand gestures to perform behaviors (or tricks). Luckily, Snowball was a quick study (or maybe it was all the treats). He mastered the commands in such a short time: potty, outside, come, sit, dance, and stay. Honestly, Snowball was more well-behaved than Robbie and Tania on some days. Snowball gave us so much love and joy for the next 13 years.

Tania

Snowball and Bambi

While we lived in San Diego, we had a dog named Snowball. He was a little white furball. When my parents found him at the pet store, they thought he was adorable and would be perfect for us. So, our parents gave him to us for Christmas. Well...actually Santa Claus brought him. In order to surprise us, they put Snowball in the garage and had us look for our gift on Christmas morning. They figured he would be crying and whining after being left in the garage, so we would be able to hear him and find him easily. But the pup never made a peep. So after a while of looking with no luck, my parents pretended like they heard something in the garage. This charade led us to go check it out. It turned out that Snowball was deaf, so he couldn't hear us searching for him in the house. He was just content to be by himself in the garage. He turned out to be the perfect pet for us. It was amazing how well he functioned regardless of his disability. He never strayed from our yard and had a really loving personality.

Snowball soon became best friends with Stacy's dog, Bambi. I'm not sure what type of dog Bambi was, but she was small like Snowball. Back then, we had a six-foot privacy fence that separated our backyards. One of the fence slats was loose, so the dogs would travel between the two yards and play together. They would choose whatever side of the fence was shaded to lay around in all day. Stacy and I would play with Snowball and Bambi by taking them on adventures and dressing them up in costumes. You know you're in a great karmic place when two family's dogs become best friends.

Snowball and the Stolen Socks

Snowball had a fetish for our socks. He never chewed them up, but he loved to steal and smell them! He would carry them around the house with him. He also never ate the dog treats we gave him. He'd take these little sausage-looking treats and hide them under our pillows. Snowball would always sleep with Robbie, but I often snuck in and stole him in the middle of the night. I can still remember the softness of his fur. Snowball never tired of cuddling with us; he loved all the attention.

A Basket for Snowball

Back and forth. Back and forth. Back and forth. I spent numerous days riding my bike up and down Dent Drive. I had this adorable bike with a little, white basket on the front. At six or seven years old, I would pretend I was Dorothy from *The Wizard of Oz*. Snowball would play Toto and ride around in the basket of my bike. Looking back, I'm sure that poor dog was hanging on for dear life as I wobbled and veered down the street, but Snowball never really seemed to mind. My buddy and I rode around Dent Drive all the time together.

Family trip to the beach

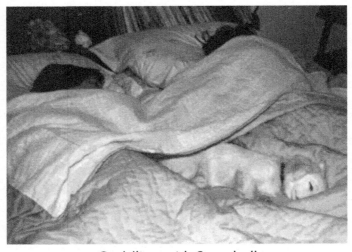

Cuddling with Snowball

Robbie playing America's game

Carol, mother of Rob and Tania, in 1975

Rob, older brother of Tania, in 1975

Stacy and Tania playing outside

Bret and his signature grin

Tania, younger sister of Rob, in 1975

Carol

It's a Zoo!

You could go to Joanie's house on any given day and find a small petting zoo. There were all kinds of animals: cats, dogs, parrots, iguanas! You name the pet, Joanie had it. I always say if you can be reincarnated, you should come back as a pet at Joanie's house. She was the local go-to person for medical information on all the animals of Dent Drive.

Carol

An Unexpected Visitor

There's a really good size canyon behind Joanie's fence in her backyard. Their sliding door on the patio had a 15 inch doggie door that swings in and out for all the pets. She was very generous with food and water for her pets, so there was always something lying around for them to snack on. Joanie's backyard had a gorgeous view of the canyon (I can see why she picked that lot). The canyon was also full of friendly critters, rattlesnakes, lizards, California Condors, squirrels, and even coyotes.

One day, Joanie and her family were all away from the home, probably at the beach. It was very quiet and calm inside. No one was in the house.

After their long, strenuous day at the beach, they come home dragging all their coolers, life vests, and wet, sandy beach towels. Dad was tired, so he immediately sat down when they got inside. The three kids did their own thing — shower, watch TV, or whatever. So Joanie was left to clean up and put everything away (remember, it's the 70's). As Joanie walks past her dining room, she sees some movement. Cats, maybe? She swings her head to the family room.

Nope, both of the cats are on the sofa with dad. She walks gingerly into the dining room. With wide eyes, Joanie turns on her heels and yells for the family to get out of the house! A skunk had decided to dine with them! Yes, skunks were in the canyon, too. If they get frightened and spray inside, you'd have to fumigate the whole house. I can't remember how they got rid of their visitor, but I do remember all of them standing on the front lawn for a while that evening.

Rob

Four-Legged Friends

We got Snowball for Christmas in 1975. Tania and I were both so excited. Snowball was deaf from birth, but we were able to train him to learn hand signals. He knew stop, come, and shake. Our friends got their dog, Happy, at the same time, who happened to be Snowball's cage mate. But Bambi (Jane and Sas's dog) was Snowball's best friend. We had a wooden privacy fence in our backyard, but somehow Snowball and Bambi were able to dislodge one of the boards and sneak through the slot in the fence to visit each other every day.

Clancy and Casey were the other dogs of Dent Drive. They both belonged to Joanie (along with all their other animals). Clancy was a wild Irish Setter. He wasn't mean, but he would jump all over you anytime you got near him. Back then, it felt like he was as big as us kids, and he probably was.

Tania

The Show

Summertime was the best because we were all out of school. There were probably 12 or 14 kids on Dent Drive. Two of the older girls were the organizers and creators of "The Show." I remember thinking how cool and pretty they both were. They were probably 12 or 13 at the time and were both tan and gorgeous. They wore makeup, had boobs, and probably had boyfriends. At seven or eight years old, I was over the moon when they asked me to be in The Show, which was to be a performance for our parents at the end of summer.

The older girls choreographed dance and acrobatic routines to songs by the Beach Boys. How iconic is that? We were living in sunny San Diego, learning dance routines to the music of the Beach Boys. The older girls would hold practices in their front yards every day. They were surprisingly so patient and caring towards us.

We donned leotards and pigtails for practice. We made human pyramids and learned how to do front walkovers, handstands, and backbends in the soft, green grass. As a child, doing cartwheels all day long brought me so much joy. We all laughed a lot and were in awe of the older girls' gracefulness. The Show ended up being a compilation of dance and gymnastics performed as duets, trios, and solos. We practiced for days on end together. Learning new stunts, memorizing the choreography, giving it our all. It seemed like we spent hours practicing almost everyday. It was summer, and we were having the time of our lives. Once we had perfected our routines, we were ready to put on The Show. We decided to do the performance in one of the older girls' backyard.

While preparing for the big day, we realized that we needed a concession stand! We had our parents make snacks, including rice crispy treats, popcorn balls, brownies, and lemonade. We sold the snacks and drinks out of the kitchen window, which conveniently faced the seating section. Yes...we sold snacks to our parents...the same parents who had made the snacks. We also charged our parents an admission fee of 10¢ per person. True entrepreneurial skills were at work at a young age.

The event was held in the evening under the stars of a perfect San Diego night. Chairs were lined up on the patio for the audience. The routines were listed in order. We were lined up along the side lines ready for our turn. Leotards on, pigtails in place, toothless smiles, giggles galore, and unbridled pride. We were so excited to share the fruits of our labor with our parents. The music was played on a portable turntable on 45s by one of the girls. As each performance began, a new record was played. One by one, we began the greatest show on Dent Drive. Our parents applauded and cheered for each routine. The parental support was critical to the success of The Show.

Camaraderie in Action

The neighborhood all worked together so well. Brothers and sisters helped one another. For The Show, we recruited our brothers to handle some of the important tasks, such as security, monitoring the gate, collecting admission, and selling snacks. It was a genius idea, and it was a huge success. The money was divided up at the end of the night to all those who helped out with The Show. Our parents still laugh at the fact that they had to make the snacks and pay admission, while we kids came home with money from our performances. How amazing it was that our parents all came to the performance and that the whole neighborhood was involved. Times like this were so remarkable to me and left a huge impression on my life. Our ages ranged widely, but everyone treated each other with kindness. I am still amazed that at a young age we were able to create and conduct an organized performance. It was the perfect culmination of summer fun.

Tania

The Boys of Dent Drive

My brother and his friends would play endless hours of tennis ball in the cul-de-sac. Tennis ball was just baseball played with a tennis ball. The boys would mark bases on the blacktop with chalk. They would arrive decked out in their knit shorts, t-shirts, and tube socks. Sporting a Padres hat or maybe even a Cardinals one. They would use wooden bats and tennis balls (because tennis balls didn't do as much damage when they hit cars or windows) and play all day long. I didn't participate in that activity, but I do remember my brother playing constantly.

Survival of the fittest was alive and well in those days. Kids solved problems on their own. If you got locked in the sewer trying to retrieve a ball (which happened a time or two), your pal would get you out or let you fend for yourself. The younger boys were in awe of the older guys who hit bombs out of the park and made incredible defensive plays. The boys would play in the morning, afternoon, and evening...only breaking for lunch and dinner. The game would continue until dark. If you had to leave the game, it continued on without you. If you were lucky, you'd come back to the game still going on. I think they kept the game going for days at a time. They loved it.

In the fall, the boys would play football. Our street was unique in that it had a semi cul-de-sac in one corner and a road that went through the cul-de-sac. In the cul-de-sac, tennis ball was the game of choice. In the road, they played football. I'm not sure who played what position, but I am sure there was an all-time quarterback and an all-time receiver. And if your ball went into the neighbor's yard, the weakest link was the all-time retriever. The neighbor lady would yell out the window, "I'm going to break your legs if you don't get out of my yard." This might sound overly rough, but her sons were also playing the same game. She was too funny.

Carol

The Girls of Dent Drive

Now let's get to the nitty-gritty of our girls on Dent Drive! The girls took dance lessons every week, and tap was their favorite. The price of the lessons? A bargain rate of $5. Every Friday after school the girls would practice on the stage at Gage Elementary School. You could hear the teacher's voice, "Shuffle, shuffle, hop, step, shuffle, shuffle, hop, step, shuffle, shuffle, hop, step. Now the other foot!" Oh my gosh, they were stars beyond your imagination! They could even heel, toe, heel, toe, slide, slide, and stomp. I think they loved their tap dancing shoes more than the practice itself. Clad in their tap shoes, which were black patent leather with a ribbon bow tie, you can hear them on the sidewalk. Clickety-click, clickety-click. The girls felt so important, and they were!

I don't remember where performances were held. But I do remember all the preparation that went into getting ready for the performances. Those were the days when we had curlers in their hair, and bows were an absolutely necessary accessory. The costumes were beyond comparison. The girls loved the day when the instructor gave them their costumes. They would all rush home and show off their costumes to each other. The girls were at different levels, so they all had different outfits, different music, and different routines. It was all so exciting for them. Makeup was not just a little bit. The dance instructor told them to make sure they had rosy cheeks, red lipstick, and bright eyeshadow. She told them, "It's hard to see your pretty faces from the audience." So, of course, they had to put on ALL the makeup.

Stacy's facial expression with her lipstick on stands out the most in my mind. She took her lipstick very seriously. Jane had her all made up, and then Stacy would FREEZE her lips. I mean really — not one movement until after the performance! She would not pucker, smile, or move them even when talking. Go ahead and try talking without moving your lips. Hilarious! She was just so afraid of messing up her lipstick.

Show Time

On the day of the performance, all the families would pile into their cars. The star performers were not to be wrinkled or messed up in any way. We finally arrived at the auditorium for the GRAND performance. Parents took their seats and anxiously waited for their daughters to dance their way across the stage.

News flash — We didn't have digital cameras back in the 70's. We might have had a Kodak Polaroid 110 with the cube flashbulbs. Just a few parents had the 35 mm cameras. The bulbs were always so bright when they went off that the girls were blinded for a moment. You never knew what you were getting in the picture either. It was going to be a surprise in a week or two, after you got them developed. You were never sure if the girls were smiling or if the picture was fuzzy from movement. What if the flashcube never went off (which happened often)? To your dismay, you would just have a big black picture. Back then, all the moms and dads would be climbing over each other, running up the dark aisle, trying to get that special shot of their daughter. Of course, they had to get close to the stage because there were no zoom lenses in those cameras. The auditorium was filled with all these flashcubes going off (or NOT).

Now the absolute best part of these grand recitals was when everyone went to Farrell's Ice Cream Parlor afterwards. About a hundred girls and all their parents packed into this one ice cream shop. Farrell's decor was that of an old-fashioned ice cream parlor with red accents, dark wood, and antique lighting. The staff was dressed in red and white striped shirts from the early 1900's. It was definitely the place "to be seen" after the recital. All the girls were in full costume, full makeup, and still in their tap shoes, clickety-clicking around in one fun-filled room. The ecstatic little girls would run around and show off their costumes to each other and their friend's parents. The siblings were more interested in ice cream and trading baseball cards than with all the social activity.

Rob

Russ Washington and Tennis Lessons

The YMCA put on a tennis instruction course, which Bret and I participated in. The lessons were held at Patrick Henry High School, the high school that students who attended Gage Elementary would ultimately attend. There was a female instructor that taught us tips and tricks while Bret and I played along with my mom and Jane for about an hour each week. Right after our lesson, there was this big, athletic guy who would begin his lesson with the instructor. Of course, my mom had to start talking to him.

We found out that he was Russ Washington, an offensive lineman for the Chargers and a Mizzou alumnus. He told us that he was taking lessons because he was in a celebrity tennis tournament and had no idea how to play tennis! We saw him a handful of times, and he ended up inviting us to come watch spring practice. I even have a picture of Bret and I with Russ. We were able to get autographs and access to preseason football, all through a connection made at a tennis lesson.

Carol

"Can I Play, Mom?"

I'm standing at the kitchen counter with my back to the door. I hear footsteps on the porch and the door opens, "Mom, mom! Hey, look at this!" Robbie is holding a blue mimeograph sheet in his hand. This was how we made copies back in the 70's. The mimeograph machine was a drum with stinky blue ink. We had to hand crank the paper to make copies of flyers or worksheets for the classroom.

With a great big smile and big round eyes, Robbie looked at me anxiously, waiting for my answer. While I was reading the mimeograph sheet he had thrust into my hand, he said, "What do you think, mom? Huh, what do you think?" It was a flyer for the Cowles Mountain Little League baseball team. I responded, "Well, I think we will show Dad when he gets home. And, I think he will like it!" It turned out that dad did love the idea. Over dinner we had a great conversation about getting Robbie a glove and a bat! Dad liked the idea so much he even volunteered to coach.

Cowles Mountain Little League is associated with so many great memories. The fields were located next to Lake Murray, near the foot of Cowles Mountain. Sas, Bret and Stacy's dad, used to walk up to the top of Cowles Mountain almost everyday. There were always great breezes through the baseball fields. If you want to know about the concession stands, ask Tania and Stacy. They spent most of the games coming to get 25¢ for candy, soda, and popcorn. They would stroll around with Snowball on a leash. Occasionally, they would chase down a foul ball. The reward for each returned foul ball was 25¢, so there were a lot of kids scrambling around for the big cash payment. Robbie would be ready to go to practice an hour before it was time to go. Bret also joined the league, but he was on a separate team because he was a year younger than Robbie. I remember Robbie playing first and second base. He had a good eye at the plate and a lot of patience. Cowles Mountain Little League was our introduction to Robbie's baseball career for the next 9 or 10 years.

Mom's Turn to Brag

There was one game in particular that stands out in my memory. Robbie was playing second base. There was a guy on first and a guy on third. The batter was in the box. The pitcher threw one smack down the middle of the plate. Obviously, the hit and run play was on. The batter hit a stinging line drive, but Robbie caught the fireball! That's one out! Some of that catch can probably be attributed to self-defense, but you don't tell your little leaguer that.

Then, Robbie's baseball instincts really kicked in. He reached out and tagged the runner who was heading to second. The umpire shot his bent arm up to indicate the runner was out. That's two outs! Robbie's hand was on the baseball, deep in the pocket of his glove. He catapulted the ball to the catcher, who was on his knees nervously protecting the plate. The runner slid. The dirt went flying. The umpire was hovering over the play. Then, the umpire pumps his arm in the infamous gesture with the most endearing words for our team and yells, "YOU'RE OUT!" That's all three outs by Robbie. Wow! I was on the bench, eyes wide open, not believing what I just saw. It was so fast. I hardly had time to process it. The team was so excited.

Then, I noticed Bob was looking at Robbie's hand. So I went over, as any little leaguer's concerned mom would. Bob said, "He hurt his middle finger. He'll be alright. We'll put some ice on it when we go home." Bob sent Robbie back out to the field. The next day Robbie woke up and his finger was twice the size it was the day before! We went to the doctor and got x-rays. Yep, it was broken! To Robbie, it was just another great story to tell the Dent Drive Gang. Everybody likes a splint or cast, right? It makes the story so much better.

Rob

America's Game

In 1978, the All-Star game was being played at Jack Murphy stadium in San Diego. We were Padres fans after having moved, but I was always a Cardinals fan first. A Cardinals fan first, then a Padres fan second. We would occasionally go to Padres games, but we all went to the All-Star Game practice that year: me, mom, Tania, Bret, Jeff, and Grandpa. It wasn't like it is now with the TV coverage of the home run derby and celebrity softball games. As I remember it, it was basically a practice the day before the All-Star Game. We got there early and stayed after so we could get autographs. Armed with notebooks and pens, we tried to attract our favorite players' attention. Tania was asking anyone who passed by for their autograph, including the worker who was restocking ice in the stadium. He said, "Do you really want my autograph?" And she said, "Yes!" So he signed her notebook with "Ice Man." I was able to get Steve Garvey's autograph by shoving an All-Star Game program and pen through his mostly closed car window, on which he scribbled his unrecognizable signature. It may be too messy to be verifiable, but I know it's real.

Back in those days, they had physical, paper ballots for you to fill out and turn in. At the time, Dave Winfield was early in his career playing for the Padres, and we loved him. Jeff and I grabbed stacks and stacks of ballots and voted for Winfield on every single one of them. We went back to the stadium and turned them all in, committing what may or may not have amounted to All-Star ballot voter fraud. I'm sure our stack of ballots really impacted the outcome of the vote.

The following year Bret won a trip to the 1979 All-Star Game in Seattle through a promotion put on by the KGB radio station. Remember the KGB Chicken? Bret and Sas ended up getting interviewed on the radio, and I recorded it on my stereo cassette tape player. I still have the cassette.

Cowles Mountain Little League

Jeff, Bret, and I also played some baseball of our own in the Cowles Mountain Little League, which had different divisions based on age. When I was eight, I was in the Caps division, which was the lowest league. The uniform consisted of a t-shirt and a baseball cap (where the division got its name). Most guys, including myself, would complete the uniform with bluejeans — mine were the Sears brand "Toughskins." I pitched and caught for the Caps. Then, there was the Minor Leagues. At that point, you were given a full uniform. In the Minor Leagues, I was on the Padres team where George S. was the coach. His son, George Jr., also played on my team. We were pretty good, and we had a lot of fun playing together.

At the fields, there was a concession stand that all the players would go to after the game to get their free team soda. I thought I was cool and would always get a "suicide," which was a mix of Pepsi, 7-Up, root beer, and orange soda.

As you progressed through the leagues, you would be required to try out for teams. For tryouts, you would bat against a pitching machine and the coaches would watch to determine their top choices. I remember George sitting behind home plate while I was hitting and saying, "Sand bag this, Robbie, just sand bag this." He wanted me to play badly so other teams would overlook me, and he would be able to draft me for his team. I ended up hitting the ball off the outfield fence to which he said, "That's not good, Rob. That's not good."

My dad and Jim coached a few of my teams. We ended up playing George's team, and I guess there was a bet between the coaches on who would win. George's team ended up winning, so one day we took my dad's government car over to George's house and started yelling over the loudspeaker. With the sirens blaring, my dad and Jim yelled, "George, come out with your hands up! We're just here to let you know that you won!" George came running out and yelled, "You guys can't be here! Quiet down! The neighbors are going to think I'm getting arrested!"

During our games, my mom kept score. She was very vocal with her support of our team, often yelling her signature line, "We want a pitcher, not a glass of water!" along with "Hey, batta, batta." Tania wouldn't pay attention to the games at all. She would be playing in the dirt with Snowball, whose fluffy, white fur would end up covered in a layer of brown dust. Every once in a while, she would run up to mom, get a nickel, and visit the concession stand.

I remember one time I was playing second base. The ball was hit to me, and it bounced up and hit the tip of my finger on my non-gloved hand. I gathered the ball back up and made the play. Then, I called time out and motioned my dad over. My finger was throbbing, but we had no extra players on the bench so my dad told me to keep playing. He said, "Get a drink of water and get back out there." I did and ended up getting a base hit and finishing out the game strong. Afterwards, we went to the hospital, got an x-ray, and found out my finger was broken. I distinctly remember thinking, "Wow, I got a hit with a broken finger." Good times in Cowles Mountain Little League.

Carol

Fun Nights at the Ballpark

Robbie's baseball team had great families — no fussing. There were parents who hosted pool parties or team nights at the San Diego Padres games. On those nights, we would go early to the games so the boys could have an opportunity to catch foul balls during batting practice. We'd then stay late, waiting at the gates for the players to leave so Robbie and Bret could get their signatures. Those were really long days at the ballpark. Fun, but long.

Stacy and Tania were not to be outdone by the boys. They wanted signatures too. So one evening, the girls ran ahead with their pens and paper. They came back very, very proud. They too had gotten signatures. We asked the girls, "Whose signature did you get?" They were so excited and yelled, "The iceman! Him over there!" Back in the 70's, ice came in giant bags for the concession stands. The iceman came from the huge freezers down underneath the stadium with big palates of cubed ice. That night he was returning the leftover ice to the freezers when his new groupies asked for his signature.

So as not to make them feel bad, we said, "Ooohhh! That's great!" Us moms laughed about it the next day over coffee.

Tania

In Our Own Little World

Playing outside was definitely something we did everyday on Dent Drive! On any given day, kids were outside playing by 8 a.m. Kids' lives during that time were different than they are now. When I was young, I took a dance class, and my brother was on a Little League baseball team. But sports and extracurricular activities didn't require the amount of time they do today. Because of that, there was so much freedom on the weekends. Since we didn't have any family in town, our friends became our family. We would play tennis ball, football, and cops and robbers. We would ride our bikes and reenact the scenes from our favorite TV shows in the front yard. It was pure childhood bliss.

The houses in California were so close together that you could stand between them, stretch out your arms, and touch both houses. We had a window in our kitchen with flat glass panes and if you turned the crank, the window opened. There were no screens because there were no bugs in San Diego. Our house was right next door to Stacy's and their family room had the same type of windows. So, I would open the window and holler over to Stacy to ask if she could come out and play. She would do the same. Our parents would check on us and call us in for dinner through those same windows. My mom would wash dishes in the kitchen and ask Stacy to play the piano, so she could listen to it while she worked. There was very little privacy, but that's not a bad thing when raising kids.

Play Pretend

Stacy and I had quite the imagination. We would play "pretend" about anything. The 70's was a time when kids' imaginations ran wild. Kids back then were allowed to daydream, imagine, create, and think up really cool things to do!

Donny and Marie were such a huge hit at the time. After watching their shows (along with the dance classes we took), Stacy and I were surely headed for stardom! Stacy's house had a fireplace with a long hearth, which was the perfect stage for our performances. It was a regular occurrence that we would use our Donny and Marie microphones and belt out songs by them, The Carpenters, or from *Grease*! Oh, to be young and carefree again. We didn't care who was in the room or in the house. We didn't care what our voices sounded like. We just knew that when we would belt out songs at the top of our lungs, we were the perfect duo. Singing, dancing, and putting on pretend performances occupied many of our days.

Other times at Stacy's house, we would just be plain silly! They had a copy of *The Guiness Book of World Records*. Inside, there was a picture of a man with the world's longest fingernails. This picture scared the crap out of us. We would grab the book, search for the picture, look at it, then scream and run away! We literally dropped the book like a hot potato and ran for our lives! A day or two later, we would repeat the drill. Find the picture, scream, run. I'm not sure why we found pleasure in this, but we sure did. Sometimes Bret and Robbie would find the picture and scare us with it. And yep, you guessed it. Scream and run! They would giggle and laugh; their mission had been accomplished.

Carol

Marathon Monopoly

How long can you play monopoly? Hours? Maybe. Days? Probably not. How about over a week? Absolutely not. Well, unless you were Robbie and Bret.

My dining room table was the place for the hot game of Monopoly between Robbie and Bret for a couple of weeks. The title of the winner went from Dent Drive Champion to City Champion, then on to State, USA, World, and finally Intergalactic Champion. The game was not continuous, but you could not disturb the sacred game board. They had school and other obligations, but the board stayed frozen while they were away. No one was allowed to use the table or disturb the board in any way.

From time to time, Bret would pop into our home and go straight to the dining room table to make sure Robbie wasn't cheating or stealing any money. He censored the board as often as he could. When he was sure that everything was on the up and up, he would walk right back out of the house. We ate every meal at the kitchen counter during that time.

Tania

Kitchens and Barbies

While my brother was playing tennis ball, Stacy and I would occupy ourselves outside too. As I said before, our garages served as our basements. Inside our garage, there was a front corner that was set up as a pretend kitchen area. Before I left St. Louis, my grandfather built cabinets out of plywood which held all my pots and pans. I also had a pretend stove. Stacy and I would go outside and fill up the pots with water from the hose. We would go into her mom's bushes, which were along the entryway of her home, and pick the berries out of her Holly Berry bushes. We would traverse the hillsides of our backyards and gather ice plants, which were succulents that grow a beautiful purple flower that blooms once a year or so. When you open an ice plant, it's kind of like the inside of an aloe vera plant — very squishy. So, of course, ice plants were the best plants to use to squish up into our homemade concoctions. We would also form mud patties because they were a joy to make.

Then, we would encircle the bottlebrush tree in our front yard and pick flowers for our concoctions too. I'm sure we were onto some type of home remedy that could have cured all sorts of illnesses. We would mix up all kinds of concoctions and play "restaurant." There were a few times when my brother and his friends, Bret and Johnny, would be playing Cops and Robbers, and they would come in and rob our kitchen. They'd dump our creations out, and we would scream and run through the neighborhood trying to catch them. All the while, our parents didn't care because we were out of their hair!

When we stayed inside, Stacy and I mostly played Barbies. When you entered my house, there was a small entryway leading to a sitting area which was our living room. We had this awful, plastic vinyl black couch. Nowadays, it would be considered retro. We would use the entire floor space to set up our Barbies because no one really walked through there. Neither one of us had a Barbie dreamhouse, but we would keep the cases our Barbies came in. We would spend hours propping open the cases, creating houses, arranging furniture my grandpa made, and setting out clothes. I think we spent more time setting up than actually playing Barbies. Of course we had the *Charlie's Angels, Six Million Dollar Man*, and *Bionic Woman* dolls in our collections too.

Our imaginations were running wild as we played *Charlie's Angels*. Oh, what a dream to be Jaclyn Smith, the most beautiful angel. Stacy was always Kate Jackson because she had a short haircut. Holly was always Farrah Fawcett because she was blonde. We would spy and solve mysteries in our backyards. The bad guys stood no chance against our makeshift guns (which were really just our fingers pointed in the steeple grip). Of course, we almost always solved the crime and caught the bad guys.

Carol

The Greatest Show on Dent Drive

One summer the older girls decided they were going to orchestrate, direct, and produce a show. It was going to be the best show ever! Probably the best show in the whole world. Okay, in the United States. Well, maybe just in San Diego. I'll settle for the best show ever on Dent Drive! I know it was one of the best summers of those girls' lives.

Everyday for about four weeks, they practiced and practiced. They made small human towers and did flips, cartwheels, splits, aerial tricks, back bends, and walkovers. Tania was about seven at the time. She loved every minute of it. We moms loved it too! We had free babysitting because the older girls would work with them everyday. Tania would come in for lunch sweating and chattering about the show the whole time she ate. And she'd sleep like a rock at night. She would excitedly exclaim, "I can do this! Watch me! I can do this split, and I can do this cartwheel." It went on and on for a month.

Where did they practice? In what conditions did they practice? Was it an air conditioned gym? Nope, not even close! How about in an air conditioned living room with carpeting? No, siree! Side note — San Diego homes did NOT have air conditioning in the 70's. Remember... it was paradise! How about comfortable gymnastics mats? Wrong again. Just plain old hard dirt with a few patches of grass and plenty of sunshine glaring down on them. Lots of hard flops and bruises. Did they care or whine? Absolutely not. Not one teeny, tiny squeak of a complaint. Just picture this: no moms, no dads, no adult instructors, no structure. Just plain creativity. A bunch of children without all that stifling adult supervision, making their synapses fire like crazy in their little brains. Never fear though, us moms were right inside ready for any emergency. Otherwise, they had free reign to call into existence the Greatest Show on Earth.

The older girls choreographed the performance to music. Back then, there was no digital stuff, just hands-on records and cassettes. So someone had to manually start and stop the music on queue. Of course the girls had costumes too. Props, including pom poms and streaming flags, were used. It was a lot of work for them. The older girls worked just as hard physically as the younger girls, if not more with spotting and supporting each girl during all the training for the big performance. The older girls even figured out how they were going to sell tickets to the parents. They drew the tickets on paper with markers, then priced them. We had a wonderful mom donate her backyard for this grand event. The backyard had to have a gate to ensure that every person bought their ticket. No one was sneaking in!

These kiddos formed a true crew. The older girls even figured out a way to include the boys of the neighborhood to participate in The Show. They now had "technical support" to start and stop the music. The show had ushers and ticket-takers. And the guys even sold all the refreshments at the concession stand (when they weren't eating and drinking all the profits, of course).

The troupe cajoled the parents into making the snacks that the boys would sell from our kitchen window. And yes, of course, the parents were expected to buy back the snacks. There were cookies, brownies, cupcakes, and pretzels. The drink choices included lemonade and the drink of the era, Kool-Aid. The paper plates, napkins, and cups were also provided by the parents.

In the cool of the evening, all eight sets of parents trekked down to see The Show. We arrived at the gate, purchased our tickets, and the ushers pointed us to our seats. Then, the concession stand opened up! Parents munched on snacks under the setting sun. Finally, the pool lights turned on — lights, camera, action!

The Beach Boys and "California Girls" blared! The little stars came charging out, makeup perfect, smiling, flipping, performing splits, doing walkovers, and dancing their little hearts out!

Carol
Neighborhood Stick-Up

The year before we moved, my father (Paw-Paw Pipe) made Tania a two-tier cabinet out of some old paneling he had in the basement. It had two sets of sliding doors and was perfect for her dishes and pot and pans. Of course, we packed it up and took it with us to San Diego. Garages on Dent Drive were for laundry, storage, and playing — not for cars. Our garage had a side door that the girls used as the entryway to their pretend home. The girls would play house and "cook" in our garage. Holly, Stacy, Tania, and sometimes other girls in the neighborhood would pick the red berries off the Pyracantha bushes and the leaves off the other bushes to put into the pots. They would pretend to cook exquisite dishes and were content playing house all day. Everything would be going perfect — nice and quiet, the way they liked it.

All of a sudden, there was screaming, yelling, and doors slamming. I hear the boys' voices say, "Put your hands up! This is a stick up!" The boys had their toy guns and were rummaging through the girls' stuff. "Gimme your money and jewelry," they yelled.

The girls were playing along, yelling, "Help! Help! Robbers! Call the police!"

So after I checked on the rambunctious situation and was convinced it was just your average run-of-the-mill neighborhood stick up, I retreated back into my home.

Rob

Newspaper Routes and Snail Picking

Bret and I ran a newspaper route for Life News through our neighborhood. We even had shirts with the newspaper's slogan, "I get it once a week." We delivered papers to about 75 houses for a few pennies each (with a ½¢ bonus for each advertisement insert). We had to buy rubber bands to wrap around the papers, which severely cut into our earnings. On top of the company t-shirts, we wore ponchos with pouches in the front and back that we could load up with papers. The best newspaper-delivery method was to fold the paper into a square, secure it with a rubber band, and toss it like a frisbee. There was a Porsche 914 on the route that was really cool, and I thought that someday I could save enough money to buy one! The newspaper was free, but Bret and I were tasked with collecting donations for the newspaper. So we went door-to-door asking people for 75¢ to support the local newspaper. We got bonuses for the donations we collected and, to our surprise, many people made the 75¢ donation.

While we tried many different modes of delivering the paper (on foot, on bikes), our favorite times were when our moms would drive us around our route. Loading up into their hatchbacks, Bret and I would hang out the back of the hatch and throw the papers from the moving car. The car had a stick shift, so the ride wasn't always smooth. One time in particular, Bret was leaning out to throw a paper when my mom accelerated a bit too quickly, causing the car to lurch forward. Bret fell right out of the back of the car and rolled down the street. He was fine, quickly jumping up and exclaiming, "I'm good!" He hopped back in and off we went. On another instance, my mom drove the hatchback right through a swarm of bees. We had to hurry and close all the windows and block all the vents before the bees could get into the car. That was not a great workday.

Bret and I ran that route for a couple of years. We would save up our money to buy packs of baseball cards or treats at the concession stand at Cowles Mountain.

In addition to delivering newspapers, Bret and I did our fair share of snail picking. A lady on Tuxford Street would pay us to pick the snails out of the evergreen bushes in her yard. We earned 5¢ for each snail we picked up. Kids would come from around the neighborhood to gather up bags of snails and collect their earnings.

Rob

The Ultimate Decision

Bret and I would ride our bikes up to the 7-Eleven (whose name was based on its hours — seven a.m. to eleven p.m.) all the time. With 50¢ each in our pockets, we'd arrive and have the ultimate decision to make. Would we use our money to buy a small Slurpee or three packs of baseball cards? The Slurpee could be either cherry or cola flavored, but the packs of baseball cards each came with a stick of gum and possibly that much sought after player. Most of the time, I would choose the baseball cards. I always wanted the Cardinals or Padres players, so we would trade our cards around to get who we wanted. I still have boxes full of baseball cards that I collected over time, some opened and others unopened. But, the decision between Slurpee or cards never got any easier for either of us.

Tania

Jackie Drive Strikes Again

As a child, I absolutely loved riding my bike. I had a great bike that had a banana seat and plastic fringes on the handles. It also had a white basket on the front which held all the important things a young girl could need: Bonnie Bell lip gloss, sunglasses, a jump rope, or my dog, Snowball.

Our house was on the corner of a giant hill. It was huge! All the older kids rode their bikes up that hill, came racing down as fast as they could, and turned left down our street to slow down. It was cool to watch them speeding and racing without a worry in the world. I wasn't allowed to go down that giant hill. I could only go up and down the wimpy hill on the other side of Dent Drive.

One day, I summoned the courage to ride down Jackie Drive. No one was around — my mom was gone, and my dad was "watching" me. I slowly walked my bike up the hill, hopped on, and away I flew. Pigtails flowing in the wind! I felt incredible; I was as cool as the older kids. Until I wasn't. I went to hit my brakes when approaching the bottom of the hill to make the left turn onto our street.

Let's just say, I was no Evil Knievel. I didn't make the turn. Instead, I flipped over my handle bars and landed on the curb. I started screaming and crying, but no one was around. Well...I think my brother witnessed my dismount, but he just looked my way and kept playing his game. In his defense, I was probably screaming and yelling all the time as a kid.

102

Then, my dad came to the rescue! He came running straight out of the garage door, lifting it up like Superman. He rushed over, picked me up, and carried me into the house. My savior! Like a good dad, he set me up on the couch with ice on my hand and waited for my mom to come home with the final verdict. She walked in the door and said, "Bob, what happened? Look at her hand! It has to be broken." He replied with a nonchalant, "Nah, she'll be alright." Mom had the final say and away we went to the emergency room. Sure enough — my hand was broken!

Moral of the story: If your gut tells you not to go biking down the big hill, you should probably listen to it and stick with the wimpy hill.

Carol

Kid Strikes Jackie Drive

Every entrepreneur starts out with a newspaper route, right? There are two in particular, who remain somewhat unknown, who started their fortunes by rolling up newspapers on my front porch. Who knew what the future would hold for them? I'm here to tell you, Dent Drive held untold phenomena for the kids who lived on that street.

The weekly local newspaper had an ad in it that said, "needing delivery boys." It was either Jane or I who found the ad. According to my recollection, I then asked Robbie if he wanted to do it. He replied, "Hmm, I don't know, mom." I added, "Well, how about sharing the job and the pay with Bret? Go see if he wants to do this." I think the pay was a whopping $8 a week (could have been for every two weeks), but that was a ton of money for a kid back then.

So Bret asked Jane if he could work with Robbie, and she gave him the green light. These junior executives then had a huge board meeting, which included discussions over shared tasks, reliability, transportation, payroll, and division of the profits (just kidding, there weren't any profits). Although, the newspaper had this sign-on bonus, which was a great incentive for the boys. They both received light blue t-shirts with black printing on the front that were at least two sizes too big for them. They were extremely excited because the shirts were FREE! Okay, so the best part of the shirt was the print on the front. It read, "I GET IT ONCE A WEEK." Yes...in large print...four inches big...bold black letters across the shirt. What kind of moms were Jane and I to let our 10- and 11-year-old boys run around with that on their shirts? Hey, it's California! Nothing else needs to be said.

The route came with a full load of benefits, including fresh air, sunshine, and a very short commute (the original work-from-home gig). Like I said, these guys were way ahead of their time.

Newsprint

The stack of papers were delivered to my front porch each week. When Robbie and Bret arrived home from school, Bret punctually scurried over. I'm sure they discussed how they were going to spend their pay. They always had a plan.

So they sat on the front porch, rolling up the newspapers and putting rubberbands around them. Do any of you remember what your hands looked like after you read the newspaper? This was way before Twitter, Facebook, Snapchat, and hashtags. Back then, you read the cartoons in the paper instead of memes on your phone. Anyway, multiply that newspaper ink a hundred fold. Their hands were black, and they always ended up with ink smears on their faces from wiping the sweat off their foreheads. The front door had handprints from them coming inside to get drinks. And their t-shirts....we won't even go there! But I loved hearing them laugh through the vented windows next to the front door. They worked and laughed for hours while rolling up the newspapers.

Delivery Time

Wednesday was the delivery day. The route they had was only 10 blocks, maybe 12. The driver of the delivery vehicle was me (working Pro Bono, of course).

First, I have to describe my car to you. It was a 1960's Volkswagen Squareback. It was a precursor to the SUV, but it was VW size. In other words, it was small. The back was a hatchback which lifted up. GREAT for delivering newspapers!

The boys put all their rolled up papers in the back of the car. I thought they could reach their arms over the back seat and grab some papers, open the doors, run, and toss. Instead, they decided they would sit in the rear with the tailgate up to eliminate opening and shutting the car doors every stop! This would enable them to jump out from the open hatch every few homes and toss the papers in the homeowners' yards. Robbie would have one side of the street and Bret would take the other. They would then hop in and grab a few more papers for the next stop, hop out, and repeat. I would drive past four homes and stop. The logistics worked really well on paper and on the level streets of Dent Drive.

Unfortunately, there's a hitch to every good plan. You know the blueprints were great, but the application found some kinks. Their route had a very long uphill street, Jackie Drive. It had an incline of about 40 degrees! Oh, did I forget to tell you the VW Squareback was a clutch, or what some people call a stick shift?

The stick shift posed a problem: You only have two feet, but you have three pedals. It gets complicated navigating a hill with stops and starts. Quick reflexes are needed, as well as attentive boys who are able to secure themselves during the jerky starts and stops. And, keep in mind...there were no seatbelt requirements in 1975.

The first stops went well. Even the first stop going up Jackie Drive went smoothly. The boys hopped in, and I started the movement of the car. In a clutch scenario, you have to quickly move off the brake to the gas pedal, and at the same time press in clutch to move to first gear. This causes the car to make a slight jerking motion.

"Everybody in?" I asked. Both boys said, "Yes!" So off we go, when I hear Robbie screaming at the top of his voice, "MOM, STOP! MOM, STOP! BRET FELL OUT!" I stopped. So did my heart and breathing. I looked in the rearview mirror and swiveled my head around. Bret was gone!

Fortunately, I then saw Bret hop up, grinning from ear to ear and laughing out loud. Bret had the best giggly laugh in the whole world. He said, "Did you see that? That was rad! I fell out and rolled down the hill!" Thank God, all he had was a skinned elbow and a great story to go back and tell all the guys on the block.

New rules came into effect immediately following that incident. We didn't need OSHA to come over. The boys were relegated to the back seat and used the doors for the rest of their newspaper delivery careers.

Hard-Earned Money

Robbie and Bret spent their hard-earned money on baseball cards at the 7-Eleven store. Eventually, they gave up their highly-coveted newspaper routes, deciding that college was a better and safer route!

Carol

Dunking Time

To Jane's dismay, I taught Stacy how to "dunk." I thought everyone knew how to dunk cookies. Why wouldn't you dunk donuts? Why wouldn't you dunk cookies? Isn't it sort of the American way?

Dunking is at its best when you take chocolate chip cookies, reach into a glass of ice cold milk with your fingers (which are probably dirty from playing outside), soak up the milk, and try to get the soggy cookie in your mouth before it gets too soggy and breaks off. I taught Stacy these steps. If it would break off, I'd say, "Get a spoon to save it from drowning!" followed by us making siren sounds like an ambulance was coming to solve the cookie emergency. Really...come on, what's better than that?

Rob

"I Swallowed a Leaf!"

My swim and dive instructor at Grossmont was named Rex. He wore his signature cowboy hat to every lesson. While probably in his late teens at the time, everyone thought he was a cool old dude. This is where I learned basic swim strokes, diving techniques, and how to tread water. I'm sure I received some sort of certification.

Sporting our Hang Ten and Ocean Pacific brand clothes (you can get these at Walmart now, which is disappointing), we'd all head over to one of the boys' houses to swim or get in the hot tub. One of the neighbor's backyard faced a then undeveloped canyon, which was cool. Clad in board shorts and t-shirts, we were California living.

Martin's family also had a pool. Once we camped out and slept on the lounge chairs surrounding the pool. We woke up in the morning to find Martin's lounge chair suspiciously empty. We looked around for a while until we found him inside, sleeping in his own bed. He had gone inside in the middle of the night and left us all out there. What was his excuse for abandoning his buddies? Apparently a leaf fell into his mouth in the middle of the night, so he went inside. Likely story.

Carol

Clandestine Poker Game

So, there we were, another peaceful day in paradise. Or so I thought. Stacy, Tania, and Holly were playing Barbies in the living room. Everyone had finished lunch. The dishes were done. It was probably around one o'clock in the afternoon. Robbie was outside playing with the boys. All of a sudden, the front door flew open. I noticed Robbie running quickly into the house, down the hall, into his room, out of his room, back down the hall, and out the door. Slam!

Hm. No, "Hi, mom." No, "I'm doing something." Nothing. That amount of stealth, quietness, and speed screams trouble to a mother's ears.

So I stood in the kitchen thinking, "What was that all about? What was he doing? What did he have in his hand? Why the speed in and out of the house? Where was he going?" Now many of you who are parents can relate to going through that litany of questions in about 2.1 seconds. I didn't have a clue what was up, but my gut told me that he was up to no good. So, like the super-cali-fragilistic-expi-ali-docious mom I was, I followed him outside. My radar was in full receiving mode.

By now, Robbie was already midway across the drive and was heading to the house next to Joanie's. To my left, Bret comes scurrying out of his house with stuff in his hands too. I surmised the situation...it just didn't look good or feel right!

I said, "Wait, wait, WAIT, boys! What are you two doing?"

Sheepishly, they replied, "Nothing, we're doing nothing."

You know that look that moms make when they know the story being told is not quite right: raised eyebrows, head cocked to one side.

I replied, "If you're doing nothing, why do you need all that money that's crumpled up in your hands?" Coins were slipping through their fingers.

Ah, guilt and fear displayed on their faces.

At that point, another cohort sauntered barefoot up the drive from his house, hands in his bulging pockets. Probably thinking, "BUSTED! Oh no, there's a mom!" But back to the guilty parties at hand, Bret and Rob. They said, "We're just going to play cards at our friend's house. It's going to be a fun card game!"

The boys who were hosting the conspiratorial activity were probably four years older than our boys. The odds were incredibly lopsided against the younger boys. I mean really...do you think the older boys weren't going to win the younger boys money and run up to the 7-Eleven with their earnings? There was no way that Bret and Robbie could possibly win any hands against these older boys. I don't know how many of the other boys on Dent Drive were involved in this casino action, but the plausibility is very high that most of them were.

So I followed them through the front door of the older boy's house. There were the culprits sitting at the table. The older boys with their deck of cards and coins on the table just waiting for young prey. If you want a mental picture, think about mini versions of a gangster poker table minus the visors, cigars, and beer mugs. That was what the table looked like to me!

Being a mom, I probably looked just like a Federal Agent with their badge displayed in their hand yelling, "HOLD IT, FBI!" With that picture in your mind, think how big everybody's eyes got when I walked in! I probably said a few mom euphemisms like, "Really? What in the world are you guys doing? What would your parents think? Don't you ever do this again!" I'm sure the tone was thunderous and much above my normal level of speech.

Needless to say, I was NOT the most loved mom on the block that day. I don't think they had gamblers anonymous yet, but I could see that's where the kids were headed. So I felt satisfied about breaking up that juvenile con-man situation. I never told the parents they had an underground gambling operation going on in their home while they were at work. I probably scared all the boys adequately for the rest of their teen years.

Fast forward to the present day. I want you to know that in all my visits to Las Vegas, I never saw any of our Dent Drive kids as dealers. Nor have I ever heard of any one of them joining the mob. Like I said in the beginning, we had some issues but avoided any serious problems. All were, and still are, great kids, and I'm proud to have had them in my life.

Rob

Contemplating the Next Millenium in an Italian Stallion T-Shirt

Sitting on the wooden fence in Jane and Sas's front yard, Bret, Keith B., Keith H., John H., Jeff, and I contemplated and talked about the year 2000. I remember that I was wearing my Italian Stallion t-shirt (it had shiny gold lettering and was handmade by my mom). This was not long after *Rocky* came out at the theaters. We marveled at the thought of it, wondering how it would ever be the year 2000. It seemed so far away. We were 23 years from the next millennium. Each of us was figuring out how old we would be. I said, "Shoot, I'll be 32 years old then, and my parents are 30 years old now." It was crazy to think that we would one day be older than our parents were at the time. Hard to believe.

At the time, we thought we would all know each other forever. It wasn't a matter of us going off in different directions or losing touch with each other. We didn't think about the year 2000 bringing incredible technological advances like in *The Jetson's*. We just thought about how old we were going to be.

Being an Italian on the West Coast

In our neighborhood, I didn't feel any racism or exclusion. Dent Drive was incredibly diverse, so there was a lot of inclusion. It just didn't matter what you looked like or what you could or couldn't do — you were included. Nobody was offended by anyone else's culture. To be quite honest, I didn't even think of the possibility of exclusion back then. We just enjoyed hanging out and having fun.

Carol

To Everything There is a Season

Nearly every Christmas and Easter we were able to go back home to St. Louis. We were so excited to see our families. As much as we loved our new neighborhood and the people in it, there were people and things back in St. Louis we were missing terribly.

First and foremost, we missed the grandmas and grandpas, and the rest of our wonderful families. While we were in San Diego, we missed several babies being born, multiple birthdays, and so many other celebrations, like our infamous Fourth of July party. In St. Louis, we would have our own show in the driveways every year. Firecrackers, sparklers, snakes, bottle rockets, fountain sprays, and the extremely loud M-80s. Jane would not have liked those (she didn't even like balloons popping). Yep, that was our Fourth of July. We hosted delicious bar-b-ques that were to die for. We had to wait all winter long before dragging out those bar-b-que pits. It was a seasonal treat, not a year-round occurrence. That in itself made it special.

Speaking of seasons, it was particularly hard for me to miss the changing of the seasons while in San Diego. There's nothing like walking in the quiet of the new fallen snow. The hush is actually deafening. The silence, except for the crunch of your boots, in the super sparkling effect of the fresh snow. The glistening that hurts your eyes. It's reminiscent of my childhood, and I truly missed it while we were in San Diego. No animals out and about, no cars driving through the neighborhoods. Just you and the silent snow — so peaceful and alluring. Just about when you become weary of winter, spring starts to show up, with its green grass and blooming flowers. In San Diego, the changing of the seasons wasn't marked by any discernible change in weather or surroundings. The shifts from winter to spring, from spring to summer, from summer to fall, and from fall to winter were just like any other day.

Planning the Big Move

Around Easter of 1979, Bob and I were talking about moving back to St. Louis. He wanted to start his own business there, so when we went back for a visit, we started shopping for a new home for the family. We thought we could 'sell' the idea of moving back to the kids by saying things like, "You get to pick out your room colors and new bedspread sets," etc. It sort of worked. We wrote a contract on a new home in the last part of March and hoped for a closing in July.

Telling our neighbors was more difficult than we anticipated. At first, the excitement about the new home covered up that difficulty. But as the time to leave grew closer, the reality of goodbyes loomed large.

Gosh, I get so choked up just writing about our goodbyes to the perfect neighbors, the perfect street, the perfect time of our life.

We ordered the U-Haul truck. The packing boxes were delivered. It was really happening! Our house on Dent Drive was filled with excitement and sadness all at the same time. In early June, I was cleaning out the cabinets (throwing out items we weren't likely to use in the next month) when this sinking feeling came and went. While I tried to sort out the items to be packed, I also tried to compartmentalize my emotions. You know, the mom is the nucleus of the family. If mom falls apart, so goes the whole family. No pressure there!

The Ultimate Beach Party

Around that same time, Jane and Joanie (God love them because I sure do) started planning this unbelievable beach party. They planned for all of the 10 families to attend the party, and every one of them was represented there in some form.

So here we were on the beach, around 10 a.m. It was absolutely one of the most gorgeous days in paradise. Joanie made one of her famous humongous salads. Several families brought Hibachi grills for hotdogs and hamburgers. There must have been at least 30 to 40 people there. Everyone brought coolers full of drinks and side dishes. Blankets and beach towels were placed all over, marking our territory. John and Mike were in charge of the Catamaran rides; they took people out all day. Beach balls, molded sandcastles, kiddos burying each other in the sand, a few dads napping here and there — you know, your typical beach scene. Unfortunately, one dad wound up with 2nd degree burns from sitting with his legs uncovered for practically the whole day. He had to go to the emergency room that night, and he couldn't go to work for a week after! We felt so sorry for him. For the rest of us, it was such a wonderful day. It was the best going away party ever!

A Gorgeous Going-Away Present

Somewhere between the beach party and moving day, there were arrangements made for one of Robbie's friends to come with us to St. Louis for a visit. All 1,792 miles, through the deserts of Arizona, the orange lands of Oklahoma, the flat lands of Kansas, Rob's friend sat in the front of the U-Haul truck with Robbie and Bob. This was back in the day when there were huge bench seats and no seat belts. After a week in St. Louis, Rob's friend was flown back to paradise. We thoroughly enjoyed having him with us on the two-day cross country trek and our first week back in St. Louis. Close to moving day, one of my neighbors (the one who would let her son come to St. Louis with us) came to my front door with a beautifully wrapped, going-away present. It was a watercolor painting of a scene of flowers in an old wooden half barrel, with the sweetest best wishes card from the family. That painting hung in my home for over 40 years. Recently, I mailed the watercolor back to her son, just in case he or his family would want a memento of their mom.

The Big Day Arrives

The U-Haul backed into the driveway just like it did four years ago. Only this time, we were loading it up instead of unloading it. The neighbors were at our doorsteps bright and early, even though we didn't recruit them. It was just mounds and mounds of love. The moms brought food and coffee. The kids were running up and down the ramp, in and out of the garage. Organized chaos is what I would call it.

The dads and boys were lifting the boxes and furniture. One dad was disassembling the dining room table so it would pack flat in the truck and not take up too much space. To this day, 45 years later, that table is still a feature in Tania's kitchen.

We also had two cars to bring back to St. Louis. We hooked one (Nellie Barrale, the VW Squareback) up to the U-Haul to tow back. Dottie Datsun, a Datsun B-210, was driven back by me with Tania and Snowball riding along. Everything, even cars, get a name in the Barrale family.

Traveling Plants

Because my friends had green thumbs, I accumulated quite a few plants during my time in San Diego. I wanted to leave them with the neighbors, but Joanie wouldn't allow that. She decided that we would pack them in the VW because they wouldn't make the trip in the back of the U-Haul. Surprisingly, they packed very well and made it back to St. Louis alive (well, some of the bigger plants' leaves got sunburned in spots while we were crossing the desert in Arizona and New Mexico).

Packing up was long and arduous. By the time we finished packing, it was mid-afternoon. We needed to get five or six hours under our belts before stopping for the night. I would be disingenuous if I said it wasn't an emotional goodbye. There were plenty of tears, hugs, and promises to keep in touch. Throughout the day, so many people stopped by to say their so longs and to drop off food for our trip. Keep in mind, this was 1979, so there weren't fast-food drive-thrus at every exit like there are now. We packed coolers and had plenty of nourishment in both the truck and the Datsun provided by our generous friends.

We had no phones to keep in contact with each other throughout the journey, so we devised a plan! It was extremely sophisticated! I would follow the truck. If it turned left, I would turn left. If it turned right, I would turn right! Simple as that. Now if Tania or I had to make a bathroom stop, I was supposed to flash my lights and the truck would get off at the next available exit. But, sometimes Bob would forget to check his rearview mirror.

I wouldn't be happy at the next stop following 15 minutes of flashing lights. Before we hit the road again, we would have a meeting to review the maps for the next stop or the exit for the next highway headed Northeast.

I want to acknowledge all the people in our neighborhood. I won't mention everyone's names here, but you all know who you are. We speak of each of you often in the most loving and jovial ways. You are the 10 most wonderful families. I could gush on and on about the Dent Drive Gang, and it would all be true. You are all present in my stories, in my thoughts, and in my heart.

Tania

Moving to St. Louis

The day that changed our lives forever was the day that my parents announced we were moving back to St. Louis. I was about nine years old when they told us. It was morning, and my parents were laying in bed. My brother and I were watching cartoons in the living room when our parents called us into their bedroom. My brother and I went to their doorway, and they asked us how we felt about moving back to St. Louis. Shrugging my shoulders, I remember thinking, "I guess I feel okay about it." Because I was so young when we moved, I didn't remember what it was like to live in St. Louis. But I also remember thinking to myself, "Why would we want to move? We're really happy here." I was confused.

I knew being in San Diego was hard on my mom because her parents and siblings were back in St. Louis. For me, my whole world was right here in San Diego. My family was here. My friends were here. At the time, I was too young to understand the importance of relationships with extended family members. My brother was very upset with my parents for moving him away from his friends and the life he had built there. We all had really strong relationships with the families in the neighborhood, and it was going to be quite the change.

My parents tried to make the move exciting for us by involving Robbie and I in the details and planning of our new home in St. Louis. Neither of my parents had jobs in St. Louis, but we were about to move across the country once more. How in the world would they do this? I would have been a nervous wreck! They selected a home to be built in a new subdivision in St. Charles County. Again, without laying eyes on the home. I still have no idea how they were able to get a loan, but they were brave, young, and could do anything. My grandparents went to watch the house be built and provided updates for my parents. Picking out the paint colors of our rooms was fun, and I was enticed by having a window seat in my bedroom. Our home was also being built on a cul-de-sac so that it had a feel just like in San Diego.

Moving day came before we knew it. I remember my dad and the neighbors packing up the moving van — chocked full of our belongings. Some things didn't make the trip, but one of our neighbors was determined to make everything fit. We had a black, wooden TV stand that just wasn't going to fit. But our neighbor took it apart and tied it to the hitch of the U-Haul truck. This time we were taking one of our cars with us. We had a Datsun, which my mom and I rode in with Snowball. My brother's friend Jeff decided to make the trip with us to see his friend's new digs, so the men drove the U-Haul. As I said, strong bonds were built on Dent Drive. I think the real reason Jeff came on the trip was that he and Robbie were having a hard time saying goodbye.

To say the least, saying goodbye to my friends on Dent Drive was not fun. My mom and Jane cried. Joanie was always strong, but I could sense the discomfort from her. Everyone was present on our last day there; all the neighbors came to bid us farewell. Joanie created a sign that said, "St. Louis or Bust" and stuck it on the truck. Through the tears and the hugs, we vowed to remain friends and stay in touch. We loaded up and left the street that held so many of my childhood memories.

It was a time in my life that I will never forget! They were the kindest, most amazing people I ever had the privilege of knowing. Our bonds have lasted a lifetime and for that I am forever grateful.

Carol

The Era

It was about 8 years ago when I met an Asian woman in yoga class. She and I would work out together. Then, we would chit-chat for a short while after classes. Through our conversations, I learned about her Japanese heritage. I relayed to her my friendship with Jane and how we have remained friends for over 40 years. This lady was very active in the Japanese Festival Week at the St. Louis Botanical Gardens when acres of the garden were transposed into the cultural setting of ancient Japan: large drums booming, original dances, poems, gorgeous silk Kimonos, white socks in wooden sandals (Zories), women with white faces perfectly made up, glowing lanterns, ornate temporary temples, and the simple Tea House.

As we continued our classes, she encouraged me to come to the festival because a renowned actor from Japan was going to do a very special dance this year at the event. She was excited about this actor honoring their request to perform here.

Although I had always wanted to go to the Japanese Festival Week, I was a little hesitant about going by myself. Eventually, I committed to go and the following Sunday I went. My friend said she would meet me at a certain time at the theatre for the grand performance. When she arrived, she bowed to me, and I returned the bow. She held a booklet out to me, explaining the story of the dance. She escorted me to my seat in the front row. I didn't expect front row seating, but I was appreciative. I bowed my head in respect that day more than I have in my entire life. It kind of felt natural to return the politeness. Before she left me, she requested I stay after the performance when she would meet me back at my seat. The dance performance was very enchanting, and the costumes were absolutely fabulous.

As planned, she came back over to me at the end of the performance and asked if I would like to go with her to a backstage room to meet her family and the star performer. Now I was getting a little uncomfortable. I was thinking, "OMG! What have I gotten myself into?" I was so shocked and flattered at the same time. I thought I was going to thank her, add a few pleasantries, then be on my way. I ended up saying, "Oh, thank you very much. I would love to go with you."

We proceeded down a long hallway into a large room. The door opened and the room was full. There was a table overflowing with sumptuous food and drinks and a collection of multi-colored orchids. People were all milling around laughing, eating, and drinking. She walked me to meet her father and mother, her husband, and her grandmother, BA-CHON. She casually pointed to her children. They were really a welcoming family.

Then, the stage door opened. The star actor entered the room. As he was wiping his sweaty white face makeup off, he was smiling at everyone. In return, they were all bowing and clapping. I did my best to imitate their behaviors. Quietly, I slipped back to the refreshments and reached for a drink. A few moments later, my friend brought the star performer over to meet me.

Picture this: I have a drink in one hand, a pamphlet and purse in the other, and a light sweater tucked under my arm. My natural behavioral reflexes kick in. My right hand wants to shake his right hand. I knew I was going to spill or drop something. Whew — saved by the bell! He bowed, and I imitated the bow, while also keeping everything in hand. Compliments were given and received, and then he moved on to more of his admirers.

I turned and thanked the lady who invited me. It was so much more than I expected. I told her how appreciative I was that she introduced me to her family and the actor. I then went on to explore the rest of the amazing exhibits at the festival. There were many more things to see! Holy Bazzoli! You should have seen and heard the outdoor drum show. It was amazing.

The most interesting portion of the festival was the Tea House. There was a sign-up sheet to participate in a Tea Ceremony. Unfortunately, I was too late for the last ceremony. I asked if I could just walk through the Tea House and was given permission to do so. I want to explain the simplicity of this Japanese Tea House culture. The decor is not loud with color or super ornate, just quiet beauty. There's an orchid on a very low table with a quiet design on the teapot and four complimentary tea cups, the kind without handles. You sort of cradle the cup in your hands and sip the green tea. Mellow music is played. There are no chairs, so you sit on very large cushions on the floor. I was saddened to have missed the ceremonial opportunity.

On the wall there was a rectangle hanging tapestry, which immediately caught my eye. It too was very simple but the characters (Japanese writing or symbols) on it were drawing me to it. I stared for a long time wondering what it said. Why was I so attracted to this nondescript hanging? Eventually, a worker at the festival came over and asked if there was something she could assist me with. I said, "I do have a question about the characters on that wall tapestry. What does it say?" She gave a very demure smile and with a twinkle in her eye she said, "ICHI-GO ICHI-E." It means, "one chance, one meeting," or, "for this time only."

This is a Japanese term that describes their cultural concept that is often linked with the Tea Master SEN no RIKYU. He redesigned the Japanese tea ceremony to utter simplicity practiced by Shuko, a 15th century monk. The modern explanation: You have tea all together and leave. Then, the next time you meet, you will be different because each of you will have had separate experiences that changed who you were at the previous meeting. So make sure each experience together is good.

That concept was very thought-provoking for me. I bowed and thanked her on my way out of the Tea House. I couldn't shake the thought, and I couldn't wait to ask my new yoga friend all about it. So Thursday class came around, and I explained my experience at the Tea House. I really wanted to know if she could write those characters for me. I wanted to frame them over my kitchen table. Sadly, she could not, but she was meeting with a friend next week who might be able to accommodate my idea. I was very hopeful.

So how does this relate to our time in San Diego? The folks of Dent Drive really exemplified the idea of one chance, one meeting, for this time only.

Through the years, Robbie, Tania, and I have had conversations about how iconic those years were and the uniqueness of our experiences in San Diego. Through those conversations I realized, as did Robbie and Tania, that those years probably had more impact on us than they did on the rest of the Dent Drive Gang. I am speaking for myself, but I think they would both agree. You're probably wondering why we think that. We all became so close during those four short years. Do you remember the song, "Don't Know What You've Got Until It's Gone" by Cinderella? That's how we all felt about moving back to St. Louis because we had all placed great value on those memories. But for the other families on Dent Drive, their lives continued as usual after we left. They had the same neighbors, the same friends, and the same lives that they always had.

Things may have changed slightly for them over time, but they had the same home base. In St. Louis, we too had a great life, but it was different than the one we had left behind. I'm just happy and amazed that we have been able to continue our friendships with the Dent Drive Gang over the span of 40 years. I think the Gang would agree with that.

It was such a great era. The kids played in the streets and yards of all 10 of the homes on Dent Drive. Doors and hearts were open. The families were on the same page of the simple right and wrong behaviors. We had "neighborhood watch" before that became a thing. As they say, "it takes a village to raise a child." Well on Dent Drive, we had a village. We had eat overs, sleepovers, all day tennis ball games, Donnie and Marie (Tania, Holly, and Stacy) singing, dancing, tag, hide and seek. Anybody could play: all day long and into the evenings or just for a few moments. The vast majority of the memories were made in and around those 10 homes.

Our children had the opportunity of a lifetime (some opportunities children these days do not have). They were kids, plain and simple. The era was one that can never be replicated.

The windows were always open. You could hear the kids playing, so their laughter often drew more children outside. You could also smell what everyone was cooking inside, not just what was being bar-b-que'd outside, while walking down the street.

The doors were unlocked. Knock, knock, "It's me," and the doors would open. Friends would appear. You could borrow an egg or a cup of sugar from next door or across the street. When was the last time you did that?

You could recognize the sounds of different people's cars. You knew when they left and when they came home. These sounds were usually accompanied by a shout of, "Hey, I'm running to the store. Could you keep an eye on the kids?"

Technology did not hold us captive yet. The kids desired real live friendships. There was genuine connection. You could see, hear, and feel how your behaviors affected others. I think there was a subliminal consciousness of kindness back then. The street's moral compasses all pointed the same way — North, up, positive.

ONE CHANCE, ONE TIME; ICHI-GO, ICHI-E.

Tania

Present Day Friendships

To this day, we've remained closest with Jane's and Joanie's families. We've attended each other's weddings. We've remembered each other's birthdays, sending cards and making phone calls. We've sent Christmas gifts back and forth. Joanie always sends my mom some kind of snail because my mom hated the snails in San Diego, especially when she stepped on them. We even created a Dent Drive Gang group text to share life's happenings with each other. Someone might send an old photograph from our childhood or a current family picture. Or a "Remember when…" text will pop up with a silly memory.

We've gone to San Diego and always have one night where we gather as many neighbors as possible for a Dent Drive reunion. The room is always filled with riotous laughter and uncontained joy! We share stories and relive the good ole days. Great people were built on that street. It produced teachers, financial advisors, pharmaceutical sales reps, store managers, mortgage lender specialists, moms, dads, doctors, authors, and really good people.

Over the years, the visits have become few and far between as our families have grown and our lives have changed. These days social media really helps us stay connected. We have the kind of friendships that you can just pick up right where you left off.

There is still a strong connection though, and always will be, between the families of Dent Drive. A 45-year connection that will never be broken.

Rob

St. Louis or Bust

I think the move back to St. Louis was hardest on me. I don't remember the exact moment in time that my parents told us it was happening, but I do remember that I didn't like it. I had made a slew of friends and was about to start middle school, but now we were moving again. I'd have to start all over. We had uprooted our lives in St. Louis, moved to San Diego, then uprooted again when we moved back to St. Louis.

Of course, all of our neighbors came over to help us on moving day — loading up the 6x4 moving truck and wishing us well. Cyn brought buckets of fried chicken from Kentucky Fried Chicken where she worked at the time. Someone made a sign that said "St. Louis or Bust," which was stuck onto the moving truck. Everyone wrote messages and signed it. *Saturday Night Live* was in its heyday, so someone wrote, "You missed *SNL* on..." We kept that sign for a very long time (my mom might still even have it).

My friend, Jeff, made the trip back with us (and stayed for about a week once we arrived). My dad, Jeff, and I rode in the moving truck, while towing the Volkswagen. My mom, Tania, and Snowball rode in the Datsun. This time we took the Southern route (through Texas and Oklahoma), and it took us two and a half days to get back to St.

Louis. I remember stopping for breakfast at a little diner in Arizona and leaving Snowball in the truck with the window cracked. When we were finished, we came outside and couldn't find Snowball anywhere. Finally, we found him under the cab of the truck, lying in the shade. Somehow he had gotten himself out of the hot truck and into the shade. We're all still baffled at how he managed that. Although my parents didn't have jobs waiting for them back in Missouri, we made the trip. They had built our new house, and Tania and I were enticed by being able to choose the color of our rooms. She chose blue, and I chose yellow carpet and walls. The house was on a cul-de-sac like our home on Dent Drive, but it just wasn't the same.

Family Feeling

Dent Drive in 1975 was such a unique place and time. We had direct access to each other's homes with a simple knock and entrance. There were so many fun days spent playing tennis ball or riding our bikes up to 7-Eleven. But what really made it special was the people; that's really what it comes down to. There was a lot of loyalty and support. There wasn't any animosity, name-calling, or put-downs. The family feeling encompassing the entire street had a comfort level that is simply indescribable. At the time, we didn't look into the future and worry about whether or not we would stay friends.

I know we were just a blip in time for the other families on Dent Drive. But we have maintained our relationships for over 50 years, and that's special. There was something inherently good in how they were all brought up. While we created new friendships back in St. Louis, replicating those years and the friendships we had in San Diego just didn't happen. Life was different.

Dent Drive in San Diego, California in the late 70's was just a remarkable place and time. There was no one event that made Dent Drive special; it was just an incredible feeling of connectedness. Some days I look out and see nobody outside in our neighborhood. I think back to Dent Drive when we were outside everyday, all day. Everyone got along. While those days are over 40 years in the past, the fond memories and warm feelings will stay with me for a lifetime.

And Now...
Epilogue by Carol Roettger

There are a plethora of stories from Dent Drive that have not been told in this book. It is amazing how much can happen in such a short time.

A few years have passed since these memories were created. The enthusiastic Dent Drive Gang grew up and times have changed. This group of 10 families produced so many amazing people. These kids (now 50+ years old) are not just prosperous, they are also high-spirited, confident achievers in the most loving and caring sense.

Us parents can proudly say we prodded, cajoled, pushed, pulled, bribed, loved, and, finally, raised these incredible humans. They have gone on to become doctors, veterinarians, elementary educators, special education teachers, administrators, office managers, CFOs, pharmaceutical representatives, executives, mortgage department managers, financial advisors, VPs, attorneys, and media managers.

And to give credit to each member of the Dent Drive Gang, they can proudly say they created their successes through hard work, sweat, determination, and perseverance. I am so proud of you all.

Character Glossary

The New Family on the Block

Bob

Father of Rob and Tania

His job transfer initiated the move to San Diego.

Carol

Mother of Rob and Tania

Known for her signature catchphrases.

Rob (Robbie)

Oldest Child of Bob and Carol

Age ranged from 8-12 during their time on Dent Drive.

Tania

Youngest Child of Bob and Carol

Age ranged from 5-9 during their time on Dent Drive.

Snowball

Beloved family dog

Best friend of Bambi.

The Family Next Door

Sas
Father of Stacy and Bret

Had a quiet and gentle manner.

Jane
Mother of Stacy and Bret

Most contagious giggle on the block.

Bret
Oldest Child of Sas and Jane

Had a unique vocabulary and ran the newspaper route.

Stacy
Youngest Child of Sas and Jane

Loved to sing, dance, and play the piano.

Bambi
Sweet family dog

Best friend of Snowball.

The Family with the Catamarans

John

Father of Cynthia, Michael, and Holly

Hilarious, intelligent, and tech-savy.

Joanie

Mother of Cynthia, Michael, and Holly

Well-known for her ability to fix and/or make anything.

Cynthia

Oldest Child of John and Joanie

Idolized by the younger girls of Dent Drive for her hip style.

Michael

Middle Child of John and Joanie

Talented sailor who loved the ocean. Full of energy.

Holly

Youngest Child of John and Joanie

Joined Stacy and Tania for The Show.

The Family that Smuggled Popcorn

Yonecko

Mother of John and Keith

Had the signature phrase
"Get outta my yard!"

John

Son of Yonecko

Played football and tennis ball with Rob, Bret, and Keith.

Keith

Son of Yonecko

Played football and tennis ball with Rob, Bret, and John.

More Kids on the Street

Keith B.

Friend of Rob

Kind and patient. Morale leader of the group.

Jeff

Friend of Rob

Traveled to St. Louis with Rob.

Made in the USA
Middletown, DE
09 September 2021